You
Can Teach Creatively

You
Can Teach
Creatively

Elizabeth Allstrom

ABINGDON PRESS
Nashville and New York

You Can Teach Creatively

Standard Book Number: 687-46728-4
Library of Congress Catalog Card Number: 72-97578

SET UP, PRINTED, AND BOUND BY THE
PARTHENON PRESS, AT NASHVILLE,
TENNESSEE, UNITED STATES OF AMERICA

For Mildred Eagan

**who thought that it should be
and that it could be**

Foreword

This book is for teachers of children.

> In day school
> In church school, vacation school, camp, and other educational programs of the church
> In the inner city
> In Head Start and similar government-sponsored projects
> In all groups where children are growing and learning

To *first-time teachers* it encourages, "Trust your ideas and those of the children as being worthy. Use them wisely, and they will lead you to sessions that sparkle and shine."

To *longtime teachers* it says, "Here are signs you may have overlooked while traveling your familiar teaching road. Some of their messages may speak to your need."

7

To *volunteer teachers* it reminds, "Cultivate the companionship of children. Look into their minds. Discover and call forth what is stored there. Rejoice that these privileges are yours. You will grow because of them."

To *potential parent-helper teachers* it urges, "Reassess your skills. They are more in number and more in demand than you suspect. Somewhere a teacher and children need them—and you."

To *all teachers* it suggests that the clues for improved teaching given by Ralph Waldo Emerson continue to be effective today. "I assume that you will keep the grammar, reading, writing in order; 'tis easy and of course you will. But smuggle in a little contraband, wit, fancy, imagination, thought."

Of course! For when these are smuggled into today's "in order" teaching, they:

Enliven the teaching
Turn ordinary sessions into extraordinary ones
Cause children to become involved participants
Direct teachers to new uses of old materials and to
    new adventures in familiar paths

For some, they also will bring the rediscovery of and new appreciation for the value and importance of the *human teacher.* No filmstrip, however effective in presenting a message in pictures, can speak the words that will give security to a bewildered child. A teacher can!

No recording, though its music or story brings much listening pleasure, can smilingly welcome a newcomer, "Your coming today is our good fortune." A teacher can!

No programmed instruction, effective though it may be to speed the learning of factual material, can express appreciation to a child for his original idea that has motivated a meaningful class discussion. A teacher can!

The brief periods that pupils spend with these several teaching devices seldom, if ever, provide for the ongoing development of the creative process as does the self-contained classroom.

Contraband, such as that suggested above, has enriched past teaching sessions and will continue to enrich future ones. Of the illustrations presented here, some have been told to the writer by teachers from various parts of the country. Some could have happened anywhere. Most are from detailed session reports written weekly over a period of more than twenty years by the teachers and supervisor of first, second, and third grades of the Riverside Church School, New York City, such reports being required from each staff member.

These sessions were for a three-hour period. The curriculum, conceived in terms of large areas of subject matter, was for grade I, Growing and Changing; for grade II, Discovering People and Places in Our City Who Are Working for a Friendly World; for grade III, Belonging to a World Family.

For all this period the writer was with these age groups, first as teacher under the supervision of Jeanette Perkins Brown, then upon Mrs. Brown's retirement, as supervisor under the direction of Dr. C. Ivar Hellstrom, minister of eduction.

This book began, therefore, not when its first word was put into place on page 1, but when a long-ago first teaching session was described in a written report. Now completed, the book is sent forth—hopefully—to stir its readers to new and deeper enjoyment in their teaching.

Elizabeth Allstrom

Contents

Teaching

*"I had a favorite teacher once. He didn't think he had
to talk all the time. Lots of times he'd laugh. And this
teacher I'm telling you about gave us lots of responsibilities."*

Marvin, age 10

Have you, a teacher of children, ever had the thought
that one fine morning upon entering your classroom you
might receive this greeting, "Hi, Mister Lewis! Guess what?
Today we're going to grade you"?

If such a welcome should be yours, would you panic?
Hoist the white feather? Quickly change the subject? Or
would you attempt a bit of make-believe bravery and
respond, "Fine. I should have thought of the idea myself"? Or acquiesce gracefully, "Please do! I ask only
that the marks you give me—good, bad, fair, or middlin'
—be what you honestly think I deserve"?

Later, knowing the results of their grading, would your subsequent actions be evidence to the class that you deserved their E for excellence? That you were trying to improve their F for failure? Would you inquire of them from time to time, "How am I doing now?"

A certain third grade once graded a teacher before either seeing or knowing him. The first teacher who came to them was without experience in teaching the longer session. He found that being present in body for more than an hour was not difficult. Keeping his mind on pupils and materials for the longer period was a different matter.

One of the children recognized the problem from experience. "My grandfather is like our teacher. When he comes to visit I see him, but not all of him. Most of him is someplace else. My grandmother is different. When she comes, all of her is there all the time. That's how I like it."

After three sessions the first teacher departed, not to return. The following week a second teacher met the class. Unlike the first, all of this teacher was there all of the time. He taught with the predictable sameness of the clock's hands moving around the hours—no encouragement of the children's ideas and few unusual ones of his own. The second teacher soon departed, not to return.

What to do next?

The supervisor hastened for a consultation with the children. "What qualifications do *you* think a teacher needs to enjoy teaching a third grade?"

Their thoughts on the subject tumbled out quickly and effortlessly as if waiting and ready for the opportunity:

"He's got to laugh."

"And not always saying to hurry."

"What I make, I want him to put on the wall."
"Sure, when we see it someplace we know he didn't throw it in the wastebasket."
"Tell him to ask *us* what *we* think."
"And when we're working, for him to work with us. Then we're doing and learning together."
"I hope he tells us stuff out of a lot of books, not just one."
"Could he do something extra with us, like on Saturday?"
"And sometime, bring us a surprise?"

The third teacher enjoyed teaching, understood children, and stayed.

A century ago teachers found guidance for their teaching in *McGuffey's Reader:* "Nor can any man teach anything well who does not think it into life before going into his classroom."

Decades later other teachers found a treasured guideline offered by George Washington Carver who, for the whole of his lifetime, never stopped learning: "A wise teacher has the gift of seeing possibilities before the pupils themselves are conscious that they exist."

In mid-twentieth century, Jeanette Perkins Brown, a supervisor of grades I, II, and III in the church school, inspired countless teachers with an observation from her long experience: "Rarely does anything of lasting value happen in the classroom, the possibility of which has not first passed through the mind of the teacher."

Today each of these directives continue to challenge and to inspire. Today, those who so easily read their words continue to find them difficult to follow. In essence each is saying, "You have an imagination. Use it to plan creatively for those you teach. Wherever your school, whatever your position in it, whatever the age of your pupils, train yourself to read between the lines of the material you teach, to find there new, exciting, and unusual possibilities for its development. Then do the spade work. Lay the foundation. Build on that foundation by adding your own sparkle, your own fresh point of view. Let the children be so caught up in the spirit of their own learning and growing that each will feel, 'I, too, have ideas. I am supposed to have them. My teacher will find ways to use the good ones along with the good ones that the other children bring.' "

Without imaginative and creative planning, sessions tend to lack purpose and momentum. With it, children and teachers feel a stirring within and recognize the stirring as good. Donald described it this way: "It tells me that I'm growing from where I already am."

Miss Wilson explained her understanding of it this way: "Whether I am a paid teacher, parent, high school student, or other volunteer come to help in the classroom, I bring my one talent plus my imagination and feel happy about them. Every teacher has these. No teacher comes empty-handed. No teacher comes with a hundred and one impressive talents all ready for immediate use. No teacher comes knowing all the answers.

"That one talent I bring to the teaching experience may be just the one that no other member of the teaching team has. 'Look,' they will say, 'our new member can:

    Cut a paper silhouette
    Do manuscript printing
    Sew a doll's dress
    Fashion wooden toys with a scroll saw
    Tell true stories remembered from childhood

Teach a game played by children in another country
Fold paper into bird shapes
Turn yarn, felt, and buttons into a picture
Smile and make everybody feel comfortable'

"Happily using the skill I have, I go on from there, ever seeking the new, the as-yet untried, the as-yet unknown."

Yes, for all growing teachers, experienced and inexperienced, the learning process is never ending. It's one of teaching's dividends. And somewhere along the way, each is almost certain to discover how to:

Add himself and his enthusiasm to the lesson topic
Encourage the children to do the same
Do research and come to know more about the lesson topic than the text provides
Create a classroom that will speak to all who enter
Make purposeful visits to the homes of his pupils

Such skills are gained through personal initiative, the expenditure of time, thought, and effort. They cannot be purchased at the store or received by mail order.

New understandings of principles of teaching and of children often come to the observant teacher from the children themselves. A kindergarten child's conversation with her mother at the close of the child's first morning's attendance at this school put certain matters in their proper perspective for one teacher.

"I like it in *this* kindergarten. It's fun. We went to the store with the teacher and bought a pumpkin, and we cut his eyes and his teeth and his mouth with a big knife, and we made that jack-o'-lantern. I got my hands all dirty with the gooshy seeds.

"The teacher put it on a table down low, and we can

look at it and smell it whenever we want to. I even put my tongue on it. Where we used to live I sat on a chair at that school like the other kids. We listened while the teacher talked. The teacher cut his eyes and made the jack-o'-lantern. Nobody helped. Then she put it high on a shelf. Nobody could touch it. Here I can talk to all the teachers and all the children whenever I want to. There's plenty of teachers and plenty of room. I don't have to be quiet. I can do what I like. I can even get wild."

For another teacher, seven-year-old Roger's exclamation on the playground brought a startling and unexpected insight about her own shortcomings.

Roger's older brother, skates already on, was waiting impatiently for Roger to get his skates strapped. When the two boys finally moved off, the older chided the younger, "Speed up, can't you?" Roger's patient reply sounded out above the rattle of their skates, "But I've told you and told you, everybody skates his own size."

This teacher later told a friend, "Suddenly my own mistakes were in focus before my very own eyes. Woe is me. Of course, no child skates the size of another. Each child in my class is unlike any other, different height, shape of nose, color of hair, sound of voice, yet I've been expecting all of them to skate the same size—Larry to handle clay with the same easy interest that Bob has; Lois to get an idea for her painting as quickly as Barbara; the whole group to listen with equal absorption to my stories. And because they don't, I am certain they feel my annoyance. Well, no matter what the source, a lesson learned is a lesson learned. So, thank you, Roger."

Teachers also learn from each other.

Two sixth-grade boys stopped one September morning at their last year's classroom to greet last year's teacher whom they had not seen all summer. Back in their own classroom before other pupils arrived, Howard told their new teacher about the visit. "We didn't hear any noise inside so I opened the door a crack. You won't believe it, Mister Springer, what we saw. Nine-fifteen, my watch says, but they've already started! Girls are in there. Our class never had girls. Everybody's painting. We never painted. Nobody even noticed us so I opened the door some more, and I said, 'Gee, Mister Bender, are you the same teacher we had last year?' He waved his paint brush at us and said, 'Good morning, boys. No, I'm not. Leadership school this summer made me different.' What do you make of it, Mister Springer?"

Word soon got around about the fifth grade's interest in painting, and their hundred percent attendance. Mr. Springer and other teachers, unable to hold out indefinitely against pressure from their classes, sought Mr. Bender. Glady he shared with them what he had learned at the summer's class. Enthusiastically he talked about materials that encouraged children's participation through the work of their hands as well as through the expression of their thoughts.

The listening teachers were in agreement about their own course of action. "None of us wants to be a replica of Mister Bender or to copy what he does. We have to take his ideas and digest them for ourselves before we can use them. Else they wouldn't work. We'd be a lot more uncomfortable trying to use something of his that wasn't really ours than we'd be if we tried walking in his shoes. Now his enthusiasm. Ah—that's different! We'd better catch that—and plenty of it—and hold on to it forever."

The discussion that followed one teacher's sharing of "The Legend of the Persian Prince" proved profitable to all present. The prince, so the legend said, was visiting in

England as the guest of royalty. One morning he was advised that on that day he was to go to the Ascot. "What is the Ascot?" he inquired. Being informed that it was a famous horse-racing meet, the prince replied, "I do not wish to go to the Ascot." He was told then that his presence at the meet was expected and proper, that courtesy demanded it. The prince remained firm in his refusal. "I shall not go to the Ascot. In my country it has long been known that some horses run faster than others."

"It's true," agreed one of the other teachers. "The winner *is* the fastest runner in any particular race. But if the prince is implying that the *expected* winner always comes in first, he is mistaken.

"Take Marcia for instance. Some of the class assumed from past experience that the paper transparency she would make would receive the honor of being the first to be displayed in the glass panel near the office door, so they didn't exert themselves on their own designs. Not so Julia. While confident Marcia dillydallied as if she had plenty of time—shall we say got out of the starting gate late—Julia moved ahead. It is her design you see in the panel this week—the first of those to be shown, an unexpected winner."

"In our class," said another, "it was Emil's idea—a late entry—that was the winner. You might say that the other ideas got 'scratched' before the race began. The class planned to enclose a clever letter with their gift of books to the children's library at the hospital, but the letters that were submitted were rejected as being 'Not very interesting,' 'Not much fun to look at or to read,' 'Too plain, no color.'

"Then Emil said, 'A rebus letter! Let's send a rebus letter! The one my grandmother sent to me isn't plain. It's fun, and I still read it sometimes. I know how to make it have a lot of color.' Emil designed the letter and with only a little help from me did all the printing. The other children painted the needed illustrations, cut them out, and pasted them in the proper spaces. It was a winner of a letter—so exciting, extraordinary, exclusive, excellent, and exactly right that I was almost selfish enough to wish it was being sent to me instead of going with the books to the children at the hospital."

"I'm wondering," said a third, "if the prince ever considered the possibility of all the horses crossing the line together, all being winners. That's what happened in our classroom when every child contributed his best thinking, his best work, his best cooperation to their play, making it a fine one and bringing equal honors to all. If you need a good slogan, that's it—'Equal honors to all. Every child crossing the line a winner.' "

Alert teachers, with antennae up and receiving sets atune, find help at quite unexpected times and places. One, listening to an after-dinner speaker, was grateful for the chance circumstance that had placed him in the audience. What he learned there he would never forget.

The speaker shared with the audience a personal childhood experience, still vividly remembered after more than fifty years. Coming with her missionary family on furlough to Boston, when she was about seven years old, the little girl was looking forward most of all to being in a real school. Her whole life had been spent in places far distant from Boston. She remembered all of them well. Now she would be in a geography class. She would learn there about many other places.

On this particular day at the new school, the little girl felt a particular happiness. She could answer *all* the geography questions the teacher asked! The teacher had distinctly said, "Answer only what you know. Only what you, yourself, have seen." Then, in orderly sequence she had asked the questions: "What city do you know?" "What river do you know?" "What mountain do you know?"

Hearing the first question, each Boston child in turn answered with monotonous sameness, "Boston." "Boston." "Boston." The little girl's answer, "Bagdad," brought from the teacher a stern look of incredulity and a stern spoken reminder that each child was expected to speak the truth and only the truth. To the second question, the Boston children again made identical responses. "Charles." "Charles." "Charles." The little girl said "Euphrates." The teacher's angry look and even angrier reminder to the little girl were this time even more upsetting. To the third question, each Boston child replied, "Blue Hill." "Blue Hill." "Blue Hill." Blue Hill was a place well known at that period by children of the Boston area. The little girl said "Ararat."

The teacher, now infuriated at what seemed the child's open disobedience, spoke harshly. "Two falsehoods, and now a third. Such places you have never seen."

"The tears and sadness of that day remain a haunting memory," the speaker said. "And to think, a book that I am preparing is the result of my writing about what I was told I did not know."

The listener, at home, continued to recall the little girl's long-ago experience. "That stern, unbending teacher did not listen to what the child was telling her. She only heard the words. Listening involves mental activity, thinking. Hearing is a physiological process. Had she given thought to the child's words, she would have recognized their truth immediately, would have felt their importance, would have woven those unusual experiences into the day's lesson to the enrichment of the entire class, would have trusted the child for further contributions in other subjects. Her failure brought needless tears to one, irreparable loss to many.

"For me, the how and why of listening have taken on a new significance. Right now, to listen well seems even more important than to talk well. Listening brings a dual responsibility. I must accurately interpret the words of each pupil. I also must accurately interpret his intent. Failure in either means that the pupil speaking his message to me may never want or try to send me another. I must be watchful for the twinkle in the child's eye—or lack of it; the smile on his face—or lack of it; his manner, and bearing. How well I listen to my pupils determines the responses those pupils will give to me."

The eager-to-improve teacher sometimes discovers, too, the wisdom of keeping atune to himself. Lacking Mr. Lewis' good fortune at being graded by his pupils or the good luck of the third-grade teacher at already possessing the qualifications required of him by a class he had never seen, he from time to time takes stock. Well aware of the touchy spots in his performance and outlook, he formulates questions relating to these areas. Then, one morning at the close of a no-trouble-all-is-fine session he tackles his list with detached and impersonal honesty. It just might include one or more of the following:

What effect did my words of greeting have on each child as he entered the classroom today?

How do Mary, Joe, and Sue feel about the way my life touched theirs? What action of mine put a new light in their eyes, a new lift to their hearts?

What word or action of mine gave the class reason to be sorry that I happened to be their teacher?

What was the "something" that reached the children

today which they could know only by being present in this class?

Which held the place of importance in my planning for today's session—to put facts and information into minds, or to present materials so that actions, feelings, and attitudes could come out?

What channel of learning did I leave open for the children themselves to discover?

Why did the class seem so eager to get to their hats and coats? Was the lesson topic too far removed from their interest and experience for them to reach? Or did I give it in a too small package of one half-hour when it deserved to be presented in a large package of many half-hours?

If I should sit down on the floor, look around, and try to view all that goes on in this classroom through the eyes of the children, what difference would it make?

To the all important question "Why am I here?" some teachers already have worked out a purpose that for them is expressive:

Not to teach boys and girls *what* to think,
not to teach them *when* or *how* to think,
but rather, to teach them to *want* to think.

Others, still in the process of searching, someday will find an equally satisfying and challenging one.

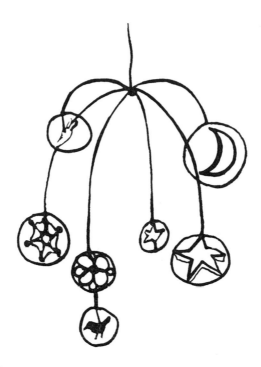

Creativity

"You mean that in all the world no one but me ever put paints together to make a picture exactly like mine? I'm the first?"

Martha Sue, age 7 1/2

A teacher from Texas enrolling in a creative activities workshop confided, "Dullness is creepng into my teaching, into my classroom. It isn't that I lack ideas. I need help in seeing possibilities for fitting them into the lesson's guidelines and having the courage to try."

"Why delay?" challenged the leader, pointing to the bright burlap, felt, yarn, and buttons on a nearby table. "Try adding your imagination to these. See what happens."

She did, and created a vivid, exciting illustration of the

previous day's story. Daily for a week this teacher put other creative ideas into painting, music, and informal dramatics and was rewarded with other surprising results. On the final day, she described her discovery in writing.

Creativity is imagination:
    a field of daisies in snow
    a grove of trees in West Texas.

Creativity is ideas:
    ideas put into action.
It is freedom:
    being unafraid to think out loud.
It is originality:
    adding a spice uncalled for in a recipe.
It is boldness:
    painting the rose blue instead of pink.
It is happiness:
    putting my own sun in the sky on a gloomy day.
It is being alive.

Creativity is being *me!*

Yes, creativity is being me, myself—no other. *Me,* a word easy to say. *Me,* a concept difficult to define. *Me,* a person with my own built-in uniqueness, my own specialness, different from that of others. Many have described the wonder of it.

Ancient Hasidic Jews had a philosophy about it: "Each man shall know and consider that in his qualities he is unique in the world. And that none like him has ever lived before. For, had there ever before been someone like him, then he would not have needed to exist."

The apostle Paul wrote about it in a letter: "Each has his own special gift from God, one of one kind and one of another."

In a poem Walter de la Mare tells children and others, too, about it:

Creativity

As long as I live
I shall always be
Myself and no other,
Just me.[1]

Creativity! It's involving my feelings, emotions, and all the dimensions of myself in whatever I do. It's putting my own spark, my own mark upon it. Then no one mistakes my work for another's or another's for mine. He knows for certain which is which, whose is whose.

"That miniature, smiling-face signature belongs to Charles. I am sure of it. Only he would think of using his initials in that clever way."

"It's Elsie's picture. No one uses blue paint in exactly the way Elsie does."

"Those clay figures of the Three Wise Men are Arnold's. I'd recognize his work anywhere."

Creativity! Every person has the capacity for it. It is not, as some suppose, the possession of a chosen few. It is given at birth to every individual. Like his breathing, his heartbeat, it belongs only to him.

When creativity is encouraged and nurtured, it grows and increases. No one can rightly predict just where it will go, what it will do. One future day it may sing itself into a silver bowl, a towering bridge, a patchwork quilt. And the world will be the richer.

When neglected or ignored, creativity often disappears, possibly never to return. Then the poem is never written, the melody never coaxed from the strings of the harp, the mathematical formula never calculated. And no one can rightly predict what the world has lost.

[1] From *Bells and Grass* by Walter de la Mare. Copyright 1942 by Walter de la Mare. Reprinted by permission of The Viking Press, Inc. and the Literary Trustees of Walter de la Mare and The Society of Authors as their representative.

Creativity! It cannot be taught or bought, lent or borrowed. But when possessed and used, its power is unmistakable.

It generates *self-confidence*. Having this, my own way of working seems comfortable and right. I have no wish to copy or imitate another's. Strings tie me to no pattern that is not my own.

It generates *courage*. Having this, I happily travel the path of my own choosing, turning here, there, as my own will directs. No other person need point the way.

It generates a *feeling* of *adequacy*. Having this, I know that success is within my reach. Mistakes I shall make, and many. But I will not fail.

It generates the *ability to see what others fail to see*. Having this, I look within a bag left on the classroom table by the carpenter finishing his work. I see not odd-shaped pieces of discarded wood. I see wood smoothly sandpapered and painted to become a miniature village, a gift that small children would enjoy.

The teacher who believes creativity to be a by-product which may or may not appear at one time or another, who does little to cultivate it in his pupils or himself:

> arrives in the classroom on the hour, marks the roll, keeps order, presents the lesson, departs.

> relies on already familiar text material to hold the pupils' interest.

> shares little of himself with the class, except his anger when something goes wrong.

> settles misbehavior with his own heavy hand.

> provides patterns and cutouts, thus assuring results that will be identical to those pictured in the text.

His teaching brings slight pleasure, small reward.

The teacher whose basic objective is to help children

cultivate the creative quality within themselves and who keeps it constantly alive within himself moves within a different framework. He

> captures and holds the pupils' interest with materials gleaned from many sources—all relating to their daily living.

> is relaxed. He has time for laughter, for conversation, for getting to know them, for finding many ways to share himself with them. His eyes and interests are ever on the children.

> has confidence that the wisdom within each child will enable him to handle his own behavior.

> encourages original work, both from their minds and from their hands and lets them feel his confidence in their ability to do it.

He proclaims to his colleagues, "There must be creative teachers, for without them, how can there be creative teaching? Without creative teaching, how can there be pupils? Without happy pupils, alack, alas, what kind of world will this be?" A world, perhaps, where children no longer will grow as unique individuals, with feelings of integrity and self-worth, where the teacher's shortcomings will be easily recognized.

With creative teaching, the many and varying interests, needs, and thoughts waiting in children's minds are released. The skills and aptitudes waiting in their fingers are put into motion. Surprises and discoveries fill the classroom. No day is without them.

Yes, the creative teacher's concern is for what happens to the children in that classroom, not for the classroom itself—its location, the up-to-dateness of its furniture and audiovisual equipment, the accuracy of its clock.

"Children must have beauty and color," he plans. "So here there will be bright cloths on tables, a prism to catch and reflect the light of the sun, leaves and bright berries brought by the children, the children's own work displayed as they choose.

"They must have space to do their work, to move about comfortably. So here furniture will be arranged to permit it. No clutter. No crowding.

"They must have materials that stimulate minds, that make hands eager to work, that invite adventures in new kinds of learning. So here there will be books, paints, paper, clay, wood, always within reach, ready for using.

"They must discover the values that come from working together. Here there will be such working together through music, writing, the playing of stories, the reading of favorite stories and poems, and the planning together for the welfare of others."

Creativity! It permeates the entire curriculum. It is not a garnish that is added on special days. Each lesson plan allows for it, encourages it, tells the teacher who reads between its printed lines, "When a topic, unrelated to the one you are presenting, touches the life of even one pupil in a special way, move toward that topic with understanding. Stay with it to a satisfying conclusion."

So, when seven-year-old Caroline, perchance, bursts into the classroom announcing, "Since yesterday we've got a baby. Maybe today I'm going to see her," and the class gathers around with eager questions, this teacher feels no guilt in postponing until another day the prepared story, song, and other activities given in that day's session plan. These are not rigid *musts* that hold him, against his own good judgment, to a particular hour on a particular day. What profit to Caroline, to the class, if he proceeds with these when the children's thoughts are in a hospital blocks away? The children will hear the story's words. They will repeat the song's words. But there will be no listening, no responding, no learning.

The teacher, therefore, moves with confidence to the new topic. The needed resources are at hand: *Poems* that speak to the many and ever changing facets of children's lives fill the pages of an always-at-hand notebook. Relevant *memories* are in his well-stocked mind. Ready-to-use *work materials* are on nearby shelves.

Should a creative teacher ever be trapped by an uninspiring text, its subject matter threadbare from tireless repetition, what then? Perhaps he courageously sets himself to the task of wresting from it or pouring into it something that will lift the material from the commonplace, that will give it vitality.

He may imagine alternate approaches to the teaching helps that confront him—ask himself, "If I were a pupil, which of these would capture and hold my interest? Which would encourage me to think for myself?"—then make his teaching plans accordingly. Which of the following permits a more creative response?

> *This:* During the first session, a co-worker brings a gift for your class—a copy of rules he made for his last year's class. Because of their effectiveness a year ago, he plans to use these same rules again this year. Have the children thank the visitor for his thoughtfulness. Add that you feel your group also will profit by their use. Copy the list on the chalkboard. Make certain that each pupil then copies his own list from it.

> *Or this:* Present your plan for class rules in some such fashion as this: "Caps usually are not worn in the classroom, but we'll be different! With the swirl of

an arm, lets each of us put on a pretend cap, a *Thinking Cap*.

"All caps in place? Each girl's thinking must produce a rule that she is certain our class will *not* need this year. Each boy's thinking will be the opposite, a rule that he believes we will need to have if we are to do our best work and to accomplish our objectives. When I see you remove your cap, it will be a signal telling me, 'My rule is now ready for discussion.' "

This: Tell the children to be creative—to paint whatever picture they want to paint. If paints are not available; tell them they will have to share the boxes of crayons. If this activity comes at the close of the session, tell them to work fast because their pictures must be finished before the dismissal bell rings.

Or this: Recall with the children the several ways that they, this year, have enjoyed stories. Suggest that each person think for a while about a particular story that he could retell today using his own painting of one of the story scenes. When the child indicates that he has such a story, direct him to the work table where he will find large sheets of paper, brushes, five or six colors of paints, and jars of water. Remind him that the painting time and sharing time are not to be hurried.

Should this teacher ever be confronted with repetitious directives that irritate him, as, for example:

Announce the work period.

Pass out the crayons and scissors.

Distribute the patterns from the packet.

Print each child's name on his work.

What then?

Perhaps he learns from the irritation. He may silently criticize those obedient teachers who conform without question to such directives, "What? Have you no originality, no ideas of your own? Or are you lazy?" and feel safe and smug himself in the knowledge that it would be impossible for him to follow such a pattern of conformity. He well knows that conformity is the enemy of creativity!

Then, in the very next session and to his dismay, he hears himself saying in words and tones he has heard not once, but week after week after week:

> "Come into the circle now. I need to see who is here so that I may mark the roll correctly."

> "It's time now for singing with the other classes. Choose a partner and remember to walk quietly through the hall."

> "Get your coats now. And let's have no fooling around."

He pulls himself up with a start. In disbelief and embarrassment the truth dawns. *Conformity has caught up with him!* To himself he offers excuses; it wouldn't have happened if I had:

> learned every child's name and had known who was who.

> trusted the children to negotiate a quiet walk through the hall without my annoying and repetitious reminders.

> always helped the children with their coats.

That day's learned-the-hard-way experience clearly points out to him that hackneyed rituals need never become the *master* of any teacher. The teacher has only to keep alert to the possibility of such a catastrophe, to use the resources within himself to transform uninspired activities into creative ones, and to remember that a constant flow of creative ideas leaves no place for conformity.

Instead of the text's "opening conversation time," let this period become one of quietness in which children can encourage new thoughts to come, can go over in their minds new responsibilities they will accept, can find new ways to share something of themselves with others.

Instead of the "wonder table" with its ever present bird's nest and seashells, invite friends to come and describe for the children mighty wonders they personally have witnessed: Mrs. Beeman, who watched a spider spin its silvery web; Mr. Robeson, who traveled beyond the Arctic Circle and watched the sun appear in full brightness at midnight to transform the scene into midday light, then move with majesty along the horizon's rim, and finally dip below it for a while, and then at midnight reappear; the Bromley twins, high school seniors, who in Kentucky's Mammoth Cave touched underground wonders—stalactites and stalagmites. These visitors and many others are available for the asking.

Instead of keeping the most exciting part of the session until all the pupils have arrived, place it first. Children arriving early and on time deserve the reward of savoring the excitement during the entire period.

Instead of the predictable schedule, have surprises. Make a *check-po!* For Korean children this bright square cloth, its opposite corners tied together, holds school books, school lunch, and cakes from the sweet-shop. For children in the class it can hold a simple surprise each week—a poem to enjoy, a familiar carol with words printed phonetically so the class may sing them as children in Hong Kong do, a letter from last week's guest, a new book of stories.

Conformity need never catch up with any teacher; the ways to avoid it are endless. Down through the ages, the superior teacher has always found ways to transmit to his pupils much more than the content of any text. With generous portions of added contraband, he moves to meet each pupil's need and interest, to enlarge that pupil's capacity for independent thinking and for many kinds of growing.

Creativity! Some may doubt its presence, but the imaginative teacher takes it for granted in every pupil, young and old alike. He offers his own inspiration and enthusiasm. Both are contagious. Either one, when caught, helps to set the conditions for creativity. Sooner or later the signs of creativity are certain to break through doubts and disbelief and bring a transformation within and without the doubting individual.

When such a breakthrough came for three teacher-pupils, they put their account of it into words and called the resulting poem "Elation":

> We did it!
> It was available materials—plus *us*.
> The materials had no form
> Until our creative abilities took hold.
>
> Then
> Tissue paper
> And reed circles
> Became twisting, turning expressions
> Of our ideas,
> Telling the story in *mobile* form.
> What a surprise!

Because of inspiration
And great expectations
Flowing from our teacher to us,
We found ourselves mastering skills
That till now
We never had thought possible.

Create?
We three?
Yes, we thought we could,
And when attention was captured
By our leader's words,
Our minds went soaring to great heights.
And ideas came
That no set pattern before
Had ever dared inspire.

Stories

"But every time you tell us a story, you have to put it inside your own head first, don't you?"

Janet, age 7 1/2

Stories! There is no substitute for them in the life of a child. With them he can take swift passage beyond his accustomed environment. Within minutes he can zoom up and away beyond the earth with the astronauts or descend into our seas with the oceanologists. He can forget his own self-centeredness while his heart reaches around the world touching others, knowing their joys and sorrows, accepting their friendships.

Whatever a child's age, stories provide food for his mind, delight for his spirit. When his routine of life is rigid and hard, they put laughter into his voice, brightness into his eyes. They shape his thoughts, give new patterns for his living, make him feel as he never felt before.

Yes, stories are springboards that project the young reader into new places and situations—away from today's clamor, confusion, and continued demands to conform to the adults' world. They take him among people who have secrets to share, bits of knowledge to teach, so that he comes away more aware of himself as he is and as he may become.

They are the gateways to treasures of the past, to accomplishments of the present, to plans for the future.

Stories have long been an instrument of teaching, both in education and religion. So it is not strange that many of today's teachers in schools and churches feel that the kernel of truth to be taught, the message to be given, can most effectively be presented within the day's story. For them, the story *is* the lesson—their most important tool.

But do these teachers often lose courage about their own storytelling skill when they compare it with that of professionals in today's mass media programs?

When they lower a needle onto a record and listen to a professionally trained voice tell the story, press a button and watch trained actors bring a story to life on the television screen, turn a knob and listen to a story, complete with sound effects, come from the radio, do these teachers think, say, cry out, "I can't compete with this"?

Or do they think, "Here is some free help. I'll learn from it. I'll take from it whatever clues and ideas seem suitable for me—those which I can make my own, which I can be comfortable with"?

Gratefully accepting this help, these teachers soon begin to acknowledge, appreciate, and capitalize on the advantages that they, themselves, hold. They are the ones who are physically present with the story-listeners. They are the ones who look them in the eye, who see them excited and on the edges of their chairs during the story's unfolding, or who see them, attention lost, minds wandering.

No storyteller on the turning record allows time for the listeners' laughter. No storyteller on television complies with the viewers' begging, "Please, please tell it again." None on the radio wait for the children's questions and give immediate answers. None smile at the small listener, who, entranced with the story, hums his own private tune while he listens. The ordinary and someday-to-be-extraordinary teacher in school and church can do *all* of these.

Story time is sharing time.

It has long been so. In ancient times and through the Middle Ages, the wandering storyteller shared his art, his way with stories, his mind the book on which they were written. In the households, villages, kingdoms, and countries to which he came, he kept alive in their telling the traditions, myths, ideals, legends, and history of the people.

Even after the invention of the printing press, which placed stories on pages of books, children wanted to hear the story and clamored to their elders, "*Tell* us a story."

A hundred years ago in America there were few storybooks for children. Public libraries were rare, as were camps or playgrounds with storytellers. But almost every family had a grandfather, an aunt, a visiting cousin who on long winter evenings gladly responded to the children's chant, "Tell us a story."

Experience reveals that everyone is a potential storyteller. No day passes without an individual relating some personal experience to another. Because it has interest to the narrator, he tells it with conviction and endless detail and wants others to be interested, too.

With the telling of only one story, he becomes a storyteller. With endless practice, much experience in the telling, plus a determined, driving desire to succeed, storytelling for him some day may become an art.

For one who wishes to tell stories well to children, continued practice is a must. Practice makes perfect. Practice gives confidence. With confidence the storyteller begins to feel free. Feeling free, he begins to share with his listeners not only the story but his own enjoyment of it. This is as it should be, for children are entitled to both. To give less is to rob the children of what is rightly theirs and to risk their indifferent responses now and in the future.

What is this story that is so important to children?

It is a narrative which gives the listener a mental picture of a little bit of life and lets him feel something about it. In the narrative, old words, which are already familiar, are rearranged in new ways. And the newness comes because the storywriter had the thought to put the words that way. With his words he tells the children something in the best way that he knows. Then he trusts them to understand it.

All good stories are constructed in the same way:

The *beginning* introduces the story people, tells where and when the story events take place. It captures the reader's interest, arouses his curiosity about a problem, and provides a clue.

The *body* describes in orderly sequence all that happens to the story people.

The *climax* discloses the solution to the problem.

The *ending* is brief and to the point. Loose ends are satisfactorily gathered together. Characters are satisfactorily accounted for.

When the storyteller lifts the words from the pages and brings them to life, he opens a window and lets the children look through to feel the joy of another's happiness, to be disturbed by another's misfortune, to wonder with those who seldom wonder, to exclaim, "Oh, I wish I had been there!"

Katie, almost eight, at the close of a story which made her wish that she had been there, gave a contented sigh, moved closer to her teacher and whispered, "Wasn't that a delicious story!" Having returned to their classroom, the teacher repeated Katie's comment to the other children. "It was indeed a delicious story. But why? What makes a story delicious?"

The answers came rapidly:

"It's got to be simple-ized—not a lot of words you don't need."

"Be interesting. You know, exciting right at the first so you want to listen all the way through to see how it's coming out."

"It's got to move along, not one word to take an hour."

"And have quick action, but not too quick. Then I can't keep my mind on what's happening."

"And not too slow with um-um-ums and er-r-r-rrrs. Then I forget what's happening."

"I get jittery if it's too long."

The storyteller that Katie heard always carries the necessary tools to make his story "delicious." Every good storyteller should possess these same tools.

Having *self-confidence*, he does not try to copy another's manner of telling. He develops a way that is his own, that lets him feel comfortable, that lets the listener feel his sincerity, warmth, and goodwill.

His *voice* is the instrument which registers the joy,

grief, or anger of the story people and makes the story seem real. He never becomes a "lady reciter," who strives for startling effects or seeks personal praise from his listeners.

To him *words* are important. Each has its own color, tone, and character. Because children's understanding of spoken words is far beyond their reading and writing knowledge of them, he is not afraid to introduce new words for them to reach to—rich, vibrant words that soon they will make their own. He never puts unnecessary words into the story. He takes out those that spoil the rhythm of the telling.

He discovers that a *pause* has several uses. It can indicate a lapse of time, build up suspense, give the listeners' minds an opportunity to catch up with the story's action or to anticipate the coming of the next incident.

His *facial expression* reflects the mood of the story people as he interprets their words and actions. It also expresses his own pleasure in the tale he tells.

He uses *gestures* if and when he feels they are needed and can be effective. He makes them seem natural and spontaneous, never forced.

Time also is an important tool. The chosen story must fit within the time period allowed for it. Neither time nor story can be stretched or compressed. A five-minute story goes into a five-minute time period. A longer story that asks for a leisurely telling must have a longer period.

Janet, at the close of one story that caught and held her interest, looked seriously at the teacher and asked, as though the thought had just occurred to her, "Every time you tell us a story, you have to put it in your own head first, don't you?"

The teacher's reply was a prompt "Yes." Later, at home, other thoughts came crowding in. "Before I put the story in my head, other information is needed. *Who* will the listeners be? Boys? Girls? Both? Of what ages? Perhaps parents also?

"*Where* will I tell the story? In a class session? In a school assembly? Around a campfire? On a playground? In front of the fire in my own home? As part of a service of worship?

"*Why* am I telling the story? For fun? Because of a particular season? To give information about children in another land? About people in Bible times? To prepare the class for taking a trip? Seeing a filmstrip? Entertaining visitors? To emphasize a particular quality in a story person's character?"

Only after these questions are answered does the storyteller begin to search for the right story. In the search he remembers that neither the first book he examines nor the second is likely to contain the appropriate story—that the one he finds may be suitable for reading but not for telling; that it may be one he cannot put his heart into.

The search may lead beyond books, magazines, his own files to people who, from their own experiences, tell him the story he seeks. Even then there may be other questions. Is it a "delicious" story? Can he tell it from the heart and with conviction? Hearing it, will the listeners reach? Come to understand something old in a new way? Have a new insight about something familiar? Be "with it"?

If the answer is "No," the search starts again. But the story is not discarded. Past experience says "Keep it. A year from now it may be exactly the story that is needed." So into the files it goes.

If the answer is "Yes," the storyteller begins to put the story in his head. He may prepare by *hearing* the story's words in their flowing from its beginning to end. Or he may prepare by *seeing* each line or paragraph on the page. Either way, he puts the story incidents into his mind, one by one in the proper sequence, then fits his own words to those of the author until he feels comfortable and confident with them. He never changes vital phrases, words of poetry, or a song within the story. To do this would rob the story of its essence, its charm, its own character.

Putting the story into one's head becomes easy only with practice. Tell the story to fifteen cushions in a row on the couch! Tell it to the flowers looking up from the garden path. Think its words while riding on the bus, washing dishes, waiting at the dentist's office. Be bold. In the practice skip from one story sequence to another until there is no hesitancy about which belongs where.

Learn well the story's beginning and end. Feel secure. Then no matter what the interruption during the time of the telling, there will be no catastrophe, no fumbling for words. The end can be handled with a flourish.

There is no best way to begin to tell a story. In the telling, stand or sit comfortably. Forget that you are Mrs. Parker, the teacher. Remember only that you are the mouthpiece through which the story enters the lives of the listeners. Wear no hat, for the children may think you are planning a sudden departure. Wear no dangling, swinging earrings or beads, for the children's eyes may become glued to their dangling and swinging. Forget personal appearance. Relax. Enjoy yourself.

Try not to give the story away in one sentence: "Today's story is about a boy whose brothers were jealous of him and sold him as a slave, but when he grew up he found them, forgave them, and brought them to live with him." Who wants—or needs—to hear more?

Get into the story quickly. When it is finished, add no explanations, no moral. If the message has not been made clear in the telling, it is too late now.

When the White Rabbit was presenting evidence at the Knave's trial, he asked directions from the King. The King said, "Begin at the beginning and go on until you come to the end, then stop." This advice is good for the storyteller, also.

Though the telling of the story may stop, the creative teacher does not stop the story. He provides many ways for its message to be held tight within the lives of the pupils who have heard it.

They may visit another class and tell the story in words they remember. They may become the story people in a play. They may put them into pictures made with paper and paints, cloth, wood, or clay. They may put them into a song. They may write a story or a poem about them.

No story need ever end with only one telling.

Informal Dramatics

"Lets us be the stockings."

Dennis, age 7

For the teacher, informal dramatics can be an exciting and rewarding way of teaching. For some it seems a magic tool. Using it they quickly discover who is who among their pupils—the bossy one, lazy one, gentle one, the show-off, the one who seldom completes work he begins, the dependable one, the natural leader, the one who says "I can't," the one who says "Please let me."

Using it they have welcome surprises. Lura, the quiet one, gains courage and speaks out, telling her ideas convincingly. Larry, chosen as usual by his friends for the hero's role, does a turnabout with his emphatic refusal. "Nicky will make the best Nicholas. He's always giving things to people, so he'll figure out how to give the gold pieces to the old man and his three daughters without getting caught. Anyway, that's his name, Nicholas."

Using it teachers make discoveries about themselves. An unaccustomed confidence, an unaccustomed faith is felt within and eventually begins to touch the children. Soon everyone in the classroom moves together in purposeful fashion in all their work.

For the children, informal dramatics can be a satisfying and different-from-the-usual way of learning. Using it they discover that big ideas come to them in ways other than by reading page 21 of the text.

Using it they find that last week's session, which held little challenge when Arthur read from the book in sing-song voice, suddenly becomes exciting today when from a pretend stage in their own classroom the whole class present the material in *their* words and *their* actions. In today's telling, each pupil, for a while, becomes a person he is not. Each one, for a while, lives in a place that previously existed for him only on the book's pages and in Arthur's repetitious words.

This adventure being successful, the children on other days play other stories. In their playing of many stories they make certain discoveries. They "get into the skins" of various people. They live and learn in many places—in India, Mexico, Africa, Chile, Palestine, in a crowded tenement home, in the spacious castle of a king. Their hearts open in appreciation of all peoples. Their horizons widen "as wide as the world is wide" in an understanding of the ways of these people.

Also, unusual and unexpected ideas pop into the children's minds. Unaccustomed rhythms find their way into their daily living. The dull routine of yesterday's learning gives way to new approaches of today and tomorrow.

Today's way—learning through informal dramatics—begins *not* when the teacher expresses preconceived notions about what the children are to do, but when the children themselves have an experience which so captures their attention, so sparks their imaginations, that they want, by means of words and actions, to relive the experience themselves and perhaps to share it with others.

In the playing, however, the children never present the event exactly as it happened. They give, instead, their own original and joyous interpretation of it. It is their playing of the event, not the event itself, that is important. Audiences recognize that only this group could play the experience in exactly this way. A part of each child—something of his own spirit that comes from within—goes into the playing and gives to it the particular mark that distinguishes it as his very own, different from all others.

In their playing, children need to know its purpose. Is it for fun? To give a message? To become a surprise gift for another class? To become part of a service of worship? Each must also have a mental picture of the person or thing that he portrays. The more detailed the picture, the truer the impersonation.

Children do not create their play upon another's demand, nor rush into its playing at the whim of the teacher. Creative work requires time, thought, care—but not perfection, for if it is perfect it is no longer childlike.

To have happy and meaningful experiences in dramatics, children do not need a drama expert, a fine building, unlimited resources, a stage with curtains, scenery, and lighting, a closet filled with costumes and props.

No! The needed ingredients are few: *time,* for creative work seldom flourishes in haste; *space,* for creative movement is more effective when not confined to one particular place; *children* with unlimited imaginative powers, for many imaginations at work assure constant variety of ideas and no repititions; *one classroom teacher,* responsive, sympathetic, enthusiastic, willing to venture, who likes teaching and knows why he likes it, for this means a friend who will always rejoice to see something come to life in the children's playing that he himself never could have thought of.

Scenery—if there is scenery—need never be the teacher's problem. Children come up with the know-how for whatever they need. They paint the background scene on two lengths of wide wrapping paper pasted together to become one large piece, attach it to the wall, and comment appreciatively to each other about its effectiveness:

> "My father could just about drive our car right across that bridge, it's that good."

> "It's so real I think I'm out there, too, with the shepherds on the Bethlehem hills under the stars."

Stage-center scenery—the princess' coach or the migrant family's worn-out car—they paint on wrapping paper, cut out the windows, then staple the pictured vehicle to a narrow wooden frame for support. Sitting in small chairs behind the coach, the princess and her attendants deftly keep it in an upright position while, with heads out the windows, they converse with passing villagers.

They paint on wrapping paper trees representing those planted by Johnny Appleseed; they cut out the trees and hang each one on an upright wooden coat tree. They tie real apples to hang down from the "arms" of the coat tree, giving the effect of apples growing on the cut-out trees and bringing smiles of approval from the audience.

Costumes—if there are costumes—never need to be elaborate. Something on the head is often sufficient to identify the character: a crown for the king, white cap for the nurse, cap with visor for the train engineer, flowing head-dress for people of Bible times. Crayons of assorted colors and white cloth of various lengths encourage the children to use their ingenuity and make what they need. When costumes are readily available there is no need, no incentive, to create them.

Characterizations and actions are simple and uncomplicated. The child plays best the role he chooses for himself, the one that has meaning for him. He quickly identifies with it, develops a genuine liking for it, and seldom is self-conscious in his portrayal of it.

The play gains in effectiveness when the children feel free to move over the entire room. Groups who experiment with such freedom come to appreciate its possibilities and seldom again willingly confine themselves to a small, specific space.

Imagine the charm, the delight in the dramatization of the French carol "Bring a Torch, Jeanette, Isabella" when not only Jeanette and Isabella, but also Marie, Suzanne, Pierre, Robert, Louis, and "all good folk of the village" come running from every corner of the room, through every door, down every aisle, carrying their make-believe torches as the song's words bid them "to the cradle come . . . Mary's calling. . . ."

Imagine the reality, the impressiveness of the scene when a group at the settlement house, caught up in the daily drama of one man's life and work in faraway Lambaréné, push out Dr. Schweitzer's hospital compound —doctors, nurses, patients, patients' families, visitors, tradesmen, animals—to all parts of the room because

50

"What Mister Doctor Albert does you can't keep in one little corner."

Lines that the player speaks are most effective when he has created them and speaks them in his own way. Then he is comfortable with them and has no fear of forgetting them. To ask a child to memorize another's words taken from a printed text is to forget that the purpose of creative dramatics is to create, not to copy. Printed words bind the speaker to a rigid pattern. He is no longer free to improvise, to add words, to change words when a just-thought-of phrase seems more appropriate than the one used previously. When participants in the play create the dialogue, each child usually knows not only his own lines but also those of the other players. Lines then become a means to move the story along rather than dependable cues to the next speaker.

During *practice*, the teacher addresses the players, and players address each other by their story names.

> *This:* Mister Riis, you are not making it clear to us why those tenement rooms are so unhealthful.
>
> *Not this:* Charlie, you need to tell in more detail about those tenement buildings and the rooms pictured in your newspaper articles.

Jacob Riis is quite willing to be more specific in his description. Charlie Austin may feel that he is being unjustly criticized in front of his friends, so will withdraw from the play.

Almost every *curriculum* provides rich resources and background for dramatic experiences. The alert and growing teacher never repeats from a year that is past. Certain that new ideas are available, he willingly searches the current material until he finds its riches. Sometimes they are concealed between the lines of the text. More often they are in plain view, calling, "Here! Here!" In either case, when the teacher finds the riches he lifts them from the pages, and his pupils, by means of dramatic play, put them into their lives and into the lives of the audiences who see their play.

Sometimes children dramatize a story spontaneously, with no direction except their own. This can happen at any time, at any place. It requires no lines, no scenery, no props, no costumes, no invited audience—only an "actor" with imagination.

Carlos was such a one. Quiet, attentive, he often smiled at the contributions of classmates, but not until the Sunday following George Washington's birthday did he volunteer one of his own.

On this day, at story time, the teacher said, "Today my story is about another George Washington—George Washington Carver. But when this George was a baby he was a slave; he had no name at all. His mother, brother, and sister were slaves, too. They were all owned by Moses Carver and lived on his farm in Missouri.

"This was at the time of the Civil War, and plunderers moving across this state often brought hardships to its farmers, ruining their crops and stealing their cattle. One night a warning came: 'Keep watch over your horses, cattle, and slaves. Raiders have been reported coming this way.'

"Mr. Carver bolted his door and locked his gates. He told Mrs. Carver, 'These night-riders are looking for strong slaves to steal and sell. They will not harm our Mary and her children.' Mr. Carver was wrong. Late that night he heard a scream from the cabin and rushed out into the darkness. Near the cabin door he found two small children. Mary and the baby were gone . . ."

The teacher paused momentarily. Just then, Carlos, eyes

flashing, leaped from his chair. Clasping the stolen baby in his arms, he mounted his imaginary horse and was off like the wind, galloping uphill and down, traveling in any direction he chose.

Rejoicing in what she saw, the teacher had no concern about this pupil's identification with the villain. At last he was participating! Without tiresome practices or a teacher's prodding, Carlos moved with confidence and assurance. His sudden, yet vivid, portrayal brought a clamor from the class for more stories about this George Washington. All wanted a turn to bring a part of his life into story play.

Ellen's portrayal of Michiko was sparked by Ronald's idea. Ellen owned a *kimono* and *geta* recently brought to her from Japan by her father. Ellen knew some Japanese New Year's Day customs. The Sunday after Christmas when she shared all of these with her class, Ronald said, "Next Sunday is two days after New Year's Day. Ellen could wear her kimono and sandals and act what Japanese families do on New Year's Day. Then all the kids would know what we know."

The children had confidence in Ellen. Ellen had confidence in the teacher. The teacher had confidence in the materials and in Ellen. So the idea began to move, Ellen, the class, the teacher all contributing. There was no practice, only the teacher's final assurance to Ellen by telephone on Saturday. Ellen needed only to listen to the story narration, then to fit her actions to the words in whatever way she chose.

Classes entering the room for the service on January 3 saw at stage left a low table (footstool) with a pretty cover and a bowl of flowers. Back of the table hung a scroll picture of Fujiyama. In front of the table were four red cushions (seats removed from the regular chairs in the room).

At stage center, four covered soup bowls were on a white cloth on the floor. At stage right the teacher sat in a chair. After introducing this first service of the New Year, she began the narration:

We go now to Japan to meet Michiko and her family. Here we see the *tokonomo,* the place of beauty in their home. And here their place for eating (pointing).

And here, coming through the door are Michiko and her family. We cannot see Father, Mother, and Small Brother with our eyes. But with our imaginations we can see them very well.

Michiko bows now to Father . . . to Mother . . . to Small Brother as they sit on their red cushions. She tells them. . . . (Michiko speaks: "May the New Year open well for you.")

It is New Year's Day in Japan. On this day every person adds another year to his age. So today is everybody's birthday. See! Michiko turns this way and that way showing her pretty birthday kimono. See! Small Brother, Akiro, wears his birthday jacket with his school emblem on the pocket.

The family moves now to eat their birthday breakfast. What is this? Akiro finds six dumplings in his soup! Because he now is six years old. Let's count the dumplings with him . . . one-two-three-four-five-six!

Now Michiko looks inside her bowl. (Michiko speaks: "Nine dumplings for me. Please help me count how old I am. One-two-three-four-five-six-seven-eight-nine!)

Father asks, "Is this family ready now to open the New Year?" Michiko, Mother, and Small Brother nod "Yes." Mother says, "I have returned the rice flour borrowed from our neighbor and the dishes borrowed from Grandmother. Nothing is in our house except what belongs to us, so I am ready."

Akiro says, "Jiro is my friend again. I told him I'm sorry I spoke angry words when he tore my book. He didn't mean to tear it. My mad feelings are gone. I can begin the New Year."

Now it is Michiko's turn. (Michiko speaks: "I accused Yuriko, my best friend, of taking a stamp from my album. Yesterday I found it on the shelf. I went to her house. 'Please forgive me,' I said. 'I am sorry.' She said, 'You still are my best friend.' My heart is happy again so I can open the New Year.")

Father tells the family, "I have paid all our debts. We owe no man anything. I, too, can open the New Year."

Breakfast over, Michiko brings paper, ink, and brushes. The family must write greetings to their friends. Michiko watches Father, then tells his message to Mother and Akiro. (Michiko speaks: "Father tells his friends, 'The New Year has opened. May God's blessing be upon your house.' ")

She now reads Mother's message. (Michiko speaks: "Mother tells her friends, 'May your New Year be one of great joy.' ")

Look! Michiko holds up one of Akiro's cards. (Michiko speaks: "All of Akiro's cards show the picture he has made of the sun. The sun is a good omen.")

Each of Michiko's cards shows a pretty design. If we were there she would teach us to make one like it. (Michiko speaks: "Look, Father! Look, Mother! I have painted our Japanese character meaning *friend*. It is on every card.")

Hear the bell? Guests at the gate are pulling the bell rope. Hurriedly Michiko takes away the cards and writing materials. Now she and Mother bow to the guests entering the door. Soon she brings a platter of sweets and passes them to the holiday visitors.

The guests are gone now and evening has come. From their places on the red cushions, Michiko and the family open and read the messages of greeting from their many friends. Father says, "Our New Year has opened well. May it continue so."

Michiko and Small Brother bow "Good night" to Father and to Mother, and all leave the room. Soon Michiko will be dreaming about the happy day when she became *nine* years old.

When the class tell their story in simultaneous pantomime and use only their imaginations, the beat of the music keeps the group moving in the same tempo. And when the accompanist at the piano catches the mood of the story's time, place, people, and action and improvises accordingly, the children discover that acting in unison with each other is fun and worth their concentration.

A fifth grade—weary desert travelers of long ago—make camp near a watering hole. To the music's rhythmic beat:

> Men *lift* heavy tents from the backs of pack animals;
>> *hammer* tent stakes into the ground;
>> *tie ropes* to the stakes holding tents securely.
> Women *dip water* from the watering hole;
>> *pour* it into jugs;
>> *lift* jugs to their shoulders, *walk* to the tents.
> Children *play tunes* on their reed pipes;
>> *dance* to the music.

Fourth-grade girls—the Egyptian princess and her maidens on a morning walk—express at the music's direction, their

> *surprise* at seeing a basket hidden among the rushes at the water's edge;
> *disbelief* at discovering a baby lying in the basket;

wonder at finding the sleeping baby to be fair of face and strong of body;

happiness at the princess' decision to claim the baby for her own.

In the resulting dance of joy, each maiden adds the rhythm of her tambourine (a real one) to that of the piano and responds to it in her own way.

Fourth-grade boys—the young Prince Asoka and his companions—practice archery in the palace garden. Across each boy's left shoulder hangs an imaginary quiver filled with arrows. In unison and to music each youth

reaches across his shoulder;

pulls an arrow from the quiver;

places the arrow in position in the bow;

pulls the bow string taut;

releases the arrow, sending it toward the target;

with hand shading eyes, *looks* toward target to determine the result.

To music the children of a third grade—migrant laborers in bean fields—in early morning

walk briskly from their shack homes;

breathe deeply of the crisp, fresh air;

hurry to the waiting bus.

In the fields they

stoop, pick, put beans in basket;

pick beans;

put beans in basket;

stoop, pick, put beans in basket.

Briefly they

stand for a moment to rest;

stretch aching backs;

rub aching legs, then continue to
stoop, pick, put beans in basket.

The day ended, they *stumble wearily* to the waiting
bus.

A second grade—neighborhood children in a crowded
city area—enjoy the safe, new playground opened on the
lot adjoining the church community center. To the one-
two beat of the piano's music they
    climb the jungle gym;
    go up—down, down—up on the see-saw;
    throw the ball—catch the ball, return—catch;
    turn the jump rope, over—under, over—under;
    jump the turning rope, run in—jump, jump—run out;
    climb the ladder—swooshhhh down the slide.

Children offer many reasons for wanting to dramatize
a particular event. Dennis probably is the first and only
one to propose dramatics as a way to solve an urgent
class problem. A visitor late in February had told the class
about the sadness in a certain church-sponsored school in
Korea during the recent Christmas season. With war in
their land, families separated, homes destroyed, food
scarce, teachers unable to provide even simple gifts, sadness was everywhere.

"If enough people help," the visitor said, "next Christmas may be different at this school."

The listening children were not long in deciding how
they would help. From unbleached muslin they cut ten
identical stocking-shaped pieces. "Big, so they'll hold a
lot." With colored crayons they drew bright Christmas
designs on each piece. But not until the children examined
the five finished stockings, machine-stitched and ready
to fill, did they realize their problem.

"Look! It's as long as I am."

"Wow! A hundred pencils won't even fill one."

Holding one of the stockings in front of him, Dennis turned this dismay into inspiration. "Lets *us* be the stockings and ask the other classes to help fill us up."

Everyone got the idea. Five immediately volunteered. As the stocking plans progressed, the other teachers were alerted to be ready on a particular day to receive five visitors. On that day each stocking, holding his decorated "self" in front of him, told his message.

> Dennis: Right now I'm an empty Christmas stocking. But I want to get full with toothpaste and toothbrushes because I'm going on a ship to bring Christmas to school children in Korea. They've got a war and need me. Will *you* and *you* and *you* (pointing) help to stuff me full?

> Crissy: See how tall and flat and empty I look on the outside? I want to feel good on the inside. Will *you* and *you* and *you* (pointing) put some warm mittens, socks, and scarves, some handkerchiefs and hair ribbons inside me so they can jump out and surprise Korean boys and girls next Christmas?

> Emma Lee said that unless she was full of marbles and jacks and rubber balls and picture books she couldn't go on the ship, so please would they fill her up so she wouldn't be left behind.

> In similar pleas, Patty asked for soap, washcloths, towels, pins, and safety pins.

> Pete asked for pencils, pencil sharpeners, colored crayons, pads of paper, and scissors.

The audiences, enchanted with the talking stockings, nodded "Yes" to every request. Some committed themselves verbally: "I'll bring pins and a washcloth." "I'll bring what I bring next week." Genuine interest made no reminders necessary. The five stockings, filled to the brim, were on their way in plenty of time.

The evaluation that follows a play given for an audience is important. It is part of the play experience itself, and not something added on. Children want to know and need to know why their play and the manner in which they have presented it brings—or fails to bring —satisfaction to themselves and to their audience. The teacher needs to know and should want to know the extent to which his involvement, interest, and enthusiasm —or lack of them—affects the play's outcome.

So, in the session following the play, when teacher and children view the playing in retrospect and express their honest opinions about it, their findings bring insights and understandings for future plays.

Evaluation requires thinking, not easy "Yes" and "No" answers.

> What factors lead you to believe that the audience got the message? Failed to get it?

> Which part of the play seemed most effective? Why? Least effective? Why? How to remedy this?

> If the play were repeated tomorrow, what changes would seem advisable? Why?

> Describe the reasons for your personal enjoyment of participating.

Two boys, almost in tears at the close of their play, were heard to comment as they left the scene:

> "Last year, in second grade, we had a good play. This year, in third grade, we did it awful."

"I know. Last year I could feel people liking it. Today I didn't feel anything."

The boys seemed to sense that to invite people to watch their play, only to have the players do less than they were capable of doing, was unfair to everybody, but at that moment they reasoned no further.

The teacher in the evaluation period later that morning was prepared for frank comments on the play. She had always encouraged them, but she was not prepared to have those comments direct her own thoughts inward.

Child: All of us knew all the lines because we had made them up ourselves. So when you had us change around to be different people that was OK. But then we quit feeling responsible for being just one person and feeling his feelings all the time. Maybe that's what made everything go wrong.

(Teacher's thoughts: Kate sensed something that certainly eluded me. But how could it, when I was there all the time?)

Child: The first practice was fun. After that it got boring. Nobody said any new words, just kept repeating what the other guys said when they were that character.

(Teacher's thoughts: If Ralph was bored, why wasn't I? Why? Why?)

Child: I could have made that one scene better with some music to guide me. Then my feet wouldn't have acted so clumsy.

(Teacher's thoughts: True, no piano. But I could have found a suitable recording. Why didn't I?)

Child: The best part of everything was painting the scenery. But nobody wants to see that play again so we might as well dump all our good work.

(Teacher's thoughts: At least I didn't hurry them with the painting. . . . But, face it I must. My heart never has been in this play. Oh, what a waste—what misery for every-body.)

At her turn to speak the teacher said, "What you have said has helped me to understand this—that the best way to be sure that the audience enjoys our play is to enjoy it ourselves. And I think to enjoy it most we must feel that the experience is fun and that we are learning from it and not being bored by it. Creating a play and partici-pating in it should make each of us a wiser and more understanding person—about ourselves and about others, too—than we were before."

> Hertha: Even in this awful play I learned something. That all good ideas aren't in the other kids' heads. My head has some, too.
>
> Carter: I wised up to know that in the play if each of us had used half the imagination he's got, the play would have turned out good.
>
> Chuck: A lot of what I learned today I thought I didn't need. But there it is. I've got it. Ready for next time.
>
> Jennifer: And Mrs. Lucas, even if you are the teacher, you have to work hard, too, like we do, to make the play good. To get wiser and understand more things.

The following evaluations, from children in an audience, were dictated to their teacher and sent in a letter. The players, with their teacher's help, found in each one a help for future plays. Their play, *The Promise*, was based on the story of that title from *More Stories to Tell*, by Maud Lindsay.

> "I understood all the words."
>
> "Right away I saw something interesting, the family sitting by the fire, and the fire looked real."

"You didn't *tell* that the harper was in a snowstorm. You let us see him in it for ourselves."

"The girls in white dresses with white balls of cotton hanging around their wrists were real dancing snowflakes."

"I felt cold in that snowstorm."

"Who could think to make a forest out of boys, each one standing straight, holding a tree branch in front of him?"

"I liked the messenger, but I don't exactly know why."

"I felt good when the harper got home safe to his wife and child and little brown dog. P.S. My friend Tiffy barked real good. He was the dog."

"I liked no curtain. No waiting. In about a week could we see your play again?"

Yes, the story the child plays, like the picture he paints, the figure he fashions from clay, the dancing steps he improvises, the story he writes is a way of enjoying again and of sharing with another something that is important to him. In it he is forever adding more to himself, finding out more about himself, entering into new sets of relationships with others and learning from them.

The story lived by acting stays long in his life. No one knows the limit of its teaching.

Art

"My teacher says just sitting in front of some clay or paints and paper won't make you an artist. You have to keep looking at them hard till you get an idea. Then you have to get excited about your idea. Then out of your own head you'll know what to do with them. That's how it is with art."

Kingsley, age 8 1/2

Today there seems to be an increasing number of forces that are working toward the standardization and regimentation of people, toward the turning of one individual into a replica of all others.

The clothes he wears, the furniture he puts in his home, the car he buys, the thoughts he thinks seem fast becoming the results of outside pressures hurled at him by advertisers, neighbors, and even friends. No longer is he the master, making his own decisions, arriving at his own convictions. Each area of his living has its category into which he is shoved, willy-nilly. In his work, one number, at his school another, at the library and bank still others, more numbers in his life than he can manage.

"Who am I today?" he wonders. "My identity as a human being is fast disappearing. Who will I be tomorrow? My uniqueness goes unrecognized. My personal feelings, emotions, skills, and abilities receive little consideration."

Those who believe that one's precious identity must never be lost brace themselves against the day when letters bringing the warm, friendly affection of friends and relatives will no longer bear the accustomed and familiar signatures, but an indifferent and impersonal X-28-493-YR2 instead.

And they wonder, "Is there anything that can help us and our children to stand firm against these many forces of regimentation and conformity? Anything to encourage the creativity within us and help us to avoid the routine and commonplace?"

Creative teachers of children know the answer and offer it with confidence—*art education*. Then, lest the questioner, at the mention of the word *art*, retreat and declare, "But I'm not an artist," they hasten to add, "Being an artist is not a prerequisite for providing meaningful art experiences. The purpose of art education is not to produce artists and craftsmen, but to stimulate the individual to want to communicate his ideas in visual form and to create an environment that impresses, inspires, and nourishes so that something happens to him as he works and learns."

To these teachers every child already is an artist within, whether he knows it or not, so they greet each child in the classroom as a unique, wonderful specimen of man, a wholly new arrangement of life, who holds all kinds of promise, who has capabilities far beyond the obvious, who has original and creative gifts to offer the world that the world would never know about if they were permitted to remain locked behind the secret door of the child's mind, as on his way he goes—following the pack.

Art is the means by which a teacher helps the child to discover that having pride in his work is a far greater reward than having a blue ribbon or other prize handed to him because another judges his work as superior.

Putting his ideas into visual form is exciting, and the creative experience of painting, of constructing a design of his own in cloth, clay, or wood, of dancing to a tune of his own making, of thinking his own words into a poem or story are all ways to help him accept himself as being a joyous part of the world in which he lives, not a cog in a wheel of sameness, a peg in a commonplace hole.

Having confidence and pleasure in his own ideas and practicing concentration as he executes the ideas will help the child to avoid the lethargy that comes from dependence on another's ideas as a substitute for his own.

The teacher of children sees art as a necessary experience for all ages. Too many there are who find one day like another, one tree like another, possibly one friend like another. For these persons art can open new vistas of living, can bring daily riches. It can help them discover pleasure in the small and in the great, find in the new and strange something that is familiar, see in the familiar something unnoticed before, appreciate the tools that are constantly in their possession and with them discover and examine the world around them.

For the child, art provides many ways for him to feel

a part of the world family to which he belongs. With paints he can create a picture of himself with a group of Japanese boys on the slopes of Fujiyama, each flying his own colorful fish-shaped kite in celebration of Boys' Day Festival.

While in his own living room he can use bright yarn and colored paper to fashion flower-like leis, surprises to be brought to tomorrow's class by a special messenger from Hawaii! One for the teacher to wear, one for each pupil, one for the day's visitor, should there be a visitor.

On another day he can be in India. In the tapestry-like picture he creates from colored cloth, bright yarn, and pretty buttons, any observer can find him there riding with a native family in their gaily decorated two-wheel cart, pulled by the family's bullock. Jogging slowly along the dusty road, the happy group is off to a festival in the next village.

Art also provides ways for the child to go back in time thousands of years and identify with people of those periods. He and his fifth grade may choose rhythmic motions to musical accompaniment as the art form in which to portray one of the basic themes of all times: the strong forcing their will upon the weak. Thoughtfully they will work out the design for the movements of the two groups: the stumbling, weary Israelites as they feel the sting of the lashes used upon them; the ruthless, heartless Egyptians as they, without mercy, drive the exhausted, dispirited ones to seek a land of their own.

His sixth grade may use dramatics as their chosen art form. In their play they will portray villagers who, in daily conversations in Joseph's carpenter shop, in their own small, flat-roofed houses, in the marketplace and on the streets of Nazareth, disclose their awareness of the various ways that a certain lad in their midst, Jesus, is growing.

Art became for one teacher a means of helping children express their feeling and understanding of worship. At the close of their first service following the summer's vacation, he said to the group of seven- and eight-year-olds, "We have been talking about being together again in this special room, and you have told me some of your reasons for being glad to be here and why this seems a special place. If you could use paints and put these ideas on paper, I wonder what color you would use to say, 'I like being quiet and listening to music'? Which color would seem best to say 'I like stories'?"

Most of the group quickly caught the idea and by their responses helped the others to understand that each painting would picture no object, but would be an arrangement of one or several colors placed in a manner that was pleasing to and had special meaning for the artist.

> "If I brought a puppy or a kitten for everybody to see, I'd use pink for gentleness to it."
> "I'd use green for thankfulness. Like for Miss Hardy and the good songs she gets for us."
> "If I got sick, I'd use purple to say I'm sorry I had to miss."

"You see!" the leader continued. "Colors speak—and in different ways to different people. To another person, blue might mean gentleness, red might mean being sorry he couldn't come. Each person's color idea is right for what he wants to tell. He never needs to copy another's. This very morning in your classrooms, paints, brushes, and paper are waiting to help you put into color the ideas you have about what we do in this room. The music Miss Hardy is playing now while you leave may help you, too.

If you are quiet and expect ideas, they are certain to come."

When the paintings were finished, each teacher, as the child told the meaning of his color design, printed his words on paper, then pasted the "story" on the reverse side of the painting.

Tony's four columns of dots, each column filled with a different color, extended from top to bottom of the page, covering it with brightness:

"The orange dots are the friends I see here.

The white dots are my thankfulness, like for this church and my home and my family and all our food.

The blue dots mean all the times I come to worship time.

The red dots are all the times I share my money and work and ideas.

See? Every time I come, I share."

Betty's large purple blob at the top of the page was crisscrossed with broad yellow lines. A wide yellow line at the bottom of the page formed a large circle which enclosed perpendicular lines, one each of gray, white, green, red, orange, black, yellow, brown.

"The round purple is all the world.

The yellow on it means the goodness reaching out to every place in the world, to parts I know, and parts I don't know.

Down below, the yellow going around is God's love for everybody.

Do you see the red people, the yellow and black people, the white and brown people?

The other marks are for all the others I don't even know about, but they're inside God's love, too."

A large red heart was at the top center of Karen's picture. Below were two purple rectangular shapes, two black squares to their left, two large yellow dots to their right. Several dime-sized dots of various colors were scattered over other parts of the paper.

"The heart means love. It's there.

The purple is for prayers—singing prayers and talking prayers.

The black is for the sadness I felt today when the new boy didn't understand about worship and made so much noise.

The small dots are for the friends I see here every time.

The big yellow dots are for the good ideas we get here and the ways we share."

In evaluating the experience, the teachers commented:

"If the creator's mood determines the success of his activity, our room had sixteen successes."

"Each picture made in our room has a freshness, a liveliness, an imaginative quality that seem to surprise even the artist. For most of them, once they laid the brush down, that was it. The picture was completed—no returning to add something here or there. To me it's important that a child feel a responsibility when he says 'My work is finished.' For he alone is the only one who has a right to say it. Integrity is involved, for his words imply, 'This is the very best that I can do at this time.' "

"All of our paintings seem to me to have a flash of something beyond the expected, beyond the ordinary. And each of them has given me an insight and understanding of the artist that perhaps I could have gained in no other way. The whole morning has awakened me to much I did not know about teaching—and learning."

"Today's experience has helped me to see that children's art is an everchanging thing—never static. As the child grows, his art also grows. It is this ever present quality of change that needs to challenge the teacher and to keep him in constant search for fresh, vital, and unusual experiences with which to fill the minds of those he teaches. A child, with mind so refreshed, never lacks motivation for his art."

Yes, the teacher who sees art as something significant and urgently necessary in the life of the child also is the teacher who understands the value of extending that experience beyond the familiar study unit and familiar classroom to fresh subjects in unfamiliar places.

One teacher, while packing work materials into a basket prior to a Saturday morning of painting in the museum's yard, told the children, "This basket is not the only receptacle we are taking. Each person is bringing his own inner receptacle. And its size determines how much of the art experience he will bring back. If your receptacle is only a tiny space in your mind, then you can bring back no more than that. If your receptacle is large, watch out! It can hold much, much more than you think."

The following day when the children arranged their several paintings in a display and for the first time noted the detailed and careful work that each of them had put into his own colorful and creative design, it was Lucy who reminded, "Our pictures are singing out to tell everybody, 'This class has baskets that are big, big, big.' "

Another teacher, leaving with his class for a late afternoon walk in an unfamiliar part of the city, advised, "Make certain that on this trip your feet are carrying your five senses as well as the rest of you! We never limit ideas for painting to those that come only through seeing."

All that was absorbed that afternoon the children stored away in their minds. Later, when impressions were put on paper, parents, visitors, and others who saw the paintings did more than see them. In their turn they, too, now walked on cobblestones and felt their rough unevenness. They, too, saw the shine of colors in a patch of oil on the street and watched the sunlight strike the west windows of tall buildings and turn them, tier after tier, into dazzling, flashing brilliance. They, too, tasted the fresh, made-while-you-wait doughnuts from a busy little shop, heard sounds of the river from busy piers, and smelled the unmistakable odors from the busy fish market.

Another class found their art subjects by looking out their windows when Bill announced, "There's lots to see down there on the river—big boats and little boats floating past." And the teacher invited, "Yes, come and look with Bill. This morning on my way here, I stopped for a while down there and watched the river and the boats. Whenever we appreciate a lovely view or respond happily to something that pleases us, a good feeling comes inside us. The whole day seems important. Keep looking from your windows until you find something that seems so interesting or exciting or important that you want to reproduce it in a way that others may see and enjoy it, too. Then come and begin your work. Paints, clay and wood, and some bright pieces of cloth and paper will be on the tables waiting for you. If you have words to create a poem or a story, my pencil will print them for you."

To this teacher, one of the finest and most enduring joys that a child—or anyone—can have comes in the act of putting something of his own choosing into visual form and in concentrating to make it his best work. For children feel deeply when they have freedom to express their ideas in their own way, with no insistence that what they make must look real or be correct or please the teacher. Then, barriers down, they reveal themselves.

At the windows, some of the children chattered about the scene below them:

"Birds swoop down over the water, then fly up to rest in trees."

"The sun sparkles the water."

"The bridge—so big! The lighthouse—so small!"

"I see two planes coming in for a landing—like two big birds slanting down, down to La Guardia."

Others looked in silence and told no one their plans.

When their work was finished and placed along the ledge at one side of the room, Bill was excited:

"Would you believe it?
All this we saw
When we looked out our windows
Our sunny windows
On the sixteenth floor!"

Yes, when children are free to express themselves and to interpret in their own way what they see, hear, and feel, art becomes a friend. They can go to it at any time. It permits them to prolong any happy experience. It is a way to tell another about the experience. It is the means for them to handle an assortment of materials, to gain mastery over them, and, in the gaining, to do independent thinking and to develop self-assurance.

How different the child's work, the results of his work, his feelings about the work when the teacher produces a coloring book and expects him to copy someone else's idea, to keep within lines that are not his own, when all of his being wants to push far beyond them.

Such an assignment saps the child's inventive power and exacts nothing of his real ability. In tackling such uninteresting, unchallenging work that is not of his own choosing, the child hears a message as clearly as if the words were spoken: "Your own ideas are not good enough. We do not need them. We do not expect them. We do not want them." So his work, identical with that of the other children, bears no mark, no spark of himself.

One glance at such a book with its unnatural, lifeless figures is, to the sensitive teacher, proof enough of its devastating influence. Since he never uses these materials, his pupils' imaginations never will be subjected to the influence of the scrawny, all-of-one-size, all-of-one-color birds, flowers, snowflakes, or what-have-you, offered on the book's pages. This teacher will keep those imaginations always sensitive to birds that soar and sweep across the great expanses of the skies, alive, gracefully moving, filled with wonder, no two exactly alike;

—always sensitive to flowers gathered in one's yard, along country roads, purchased at the florist's shop—blossoms that startle small fingers by the softness of their texture; that startle bright eyes by the boldness of their color; each blossom different from the others;

—always sensitive to the feel and delight of snowflakes blowing on faces, falling on mittens and caps, on city streets and country roads, transforming a familiar world into a scene of sparkling, fairy-like whiteness; and among the millions of falling star-shaped flakes, each different from all the others.

Children who cut out patterns devised by another person and fill them with a color according to the whim of another, also hear an unspoken message: "Take it easy.

You do not need to think. We have done your thinking for you."

The use of patterns makes the child's mind dependent, inflexible, with no desire to leap forward and tackle whatever the situation demands. Their use destroys his sense of perception, lets no part of him be visible except his skill—or lack of it—with scissors.

Their use never rewards him, the teacher, or the other children with a surprise, never lets them behold something that is different from what they have seen before. Using them, the child becomes more dependent in his thinking so that, whatever his need, he comes to expect that help in how-to-do-it always will be provided for him, either in a book or by a person. And all the while, he is unaware that his own growth depends in great measure on his thinking and doing for himself and that the needed power lies within his own mind, unused.

Art education, the touchstone of good teaching in every kind of school, helps every child discover and use this power.

Music

It isn't only the many pipes
It isn't only the rushing wind.
It isn't even the black keys
And the shutters opening and closing.

It's the music inside the player.
It's the music inside the composer.
It's the music inside the listener.
Inside music coming out.

Bettina, age 8 1/2

The third grade would long remember their visit to the organ. Being permitted to touch the fine instrument was treat enough, but others also awaited them.

At the invitation of Mr. Moore, the organist, the children stood close beside him at the console. There they examined the stops and pistons. There they sounded the keys and pedals. There Adam handed Mr. Moore their list of questions. "We wrote them on paper in case we forgot what we wanted to know." Mr. Moore answered each question, then told the visitors, "The music that I will play for you was composed more than a hundred years ago. Now you will join the countless other persons who have enjoyed it and will remember it."

This was the best treat of all. Watching Mr. Moore's hands move smoothly over all the keyboards, bringing the music from black keys and white keys. Watching his feet move quickly on the pedals. Without looking, Mr. Moore knew instantly the position of each pedal, knew which foot to use to reach the needed one.

When the music stopped, Dwight thought of another question. "Music's only music when you *hear* it. Right?"

"Partly right," Mr. Moore replied, holding the music sheets for the children to see. "The composer knows how his music sounds without hearing it played on an instrument. Others need to hear it. So the composer makes signs like these for the musician to follow so his music can be heard. But do these black marks let you hear music? Do they tell you, Sing? Dance? No! But when they are lifted off the paper, brought to life on some instrument—ah! Then you hear them call and you do what the music says."

Again Mr. Moore's hands and feet moved over keys and pedals. The familiar tune that he played called, "Sing!" The children obeyed. Now *they* were the music-makers.

Their song ended, the children climbed with their friend to places high above the organ. Here the organ's pipes stood silent and still, levers and rods that controlled them—motionless. Only upon signal from the musician at the console would the levers move again, the shutters of the pipes open and close, the music be heard.

The children often talked about the organ. Listening to its music, playing its keys, singing its song now were a happy part of their lives.

Bettina's thoughts about the organ include her phrase "Inside music coming out." It is for this reason that children must have many experiences with music—to let the "inside music" come out.

When children do not have these experiences, sometimes it is because their classroom teacher, lacking professional training in music, is reluctant or a bit afraid to venture in providing them. For some reluctant teachers, the nearby presence of a music resource person may give needed confidence for adventuring. For others, knowing that professional help is available may stifle initiative and produce a "follower," not an "adventurer." Music that another suggests or that is used because another suggests it seldom is completely successful. It is not his own; it lacks his spark—his mark.

The teacher who is himself convinced that music is an important experience for children and is himself excited about bringing it to them finds that ideas come to him from many sources. Lo! On his own doorstep some are waiting. Lo! In his own mind he finds others. Because he knows the interests, needs, and abilities of his pupils, he senses which of these will be successful immediately, which should be saved for a future time, which may never be right for his particular situation.

He cares little that his choices are not described in a textbook, do not appear on a list approved by specialists. His own confidence and enthusiasm about their rightness for this time, this place, these pupils, need no approval, no confirming "Yes" from others.

One convinced teacher, who opened his eyes and

looked around him, found on his doorstep a stained-glass window that pictured the history of music.

To see a stained-glass window with the sunlight streaming through its many colors, the rainbow hues falling across the floor in front of it, quickens any heart at any time. For one of this teacher's pupils, the first view of the music window brought her on tiptoes exclaiming, "It's like gay, dancing flowers—and gold all around." For his entire class the window became a stepping stone to fresh and unexpected musical experiences.

Simple tom-tom drums and slender reed pipes began the pictured story. The noble and complex pipe organ ended it. Its other pictures included:

a Roman water organ;
a pianoforte;
Belgian carillon bells;
David playing his harp before King Saul;
Martin Luther and his family singing together;
a translator putting the book of Psalms into
    another language;
dancers interpreting music through rhythmic move-
    ments.

From the window children moved out to observe, learn about, make, interpret, enjoy music in many ways. They raised questions and found answers. They used minds and imaginations in ways that brought music very close.

From the window their teacher, untrained in music, yet convinced of its importance in the lives of children, grew confident that no class of his would ever be deprived of it.

Listening to music can be more than listening.

A first-grade teacher invited, "Find a comfortable place this spring morning to listen to spring music. Robin once told us that she listens best when she closes her eyes. You may be surprised at what the music lets you hear. Listen carefully. Then I will ask, 'What did you hear, Virginia? What did you hear Tuck? Everybody?' "

When the selection of spring music was finished, the sharing began:

Virginia heard the lullaby a mother was singing to her baby;

Tom heard many birds flying overhead, high in the air;

Ken heard waves of water swooshing on the lake;

Jimmy heard leaves waving in the breeze;

Robin heard a mother cat moving softly, looking for a place to put her kittens;

Tim heard leaves—lots of leaves—shimmering;

Peggy heard tree branches twisting and turning in the wind;

Bobby heard water in a brook gurgling over rocks.

The teacher said, "Spring music must have a kind of magic. It lets each person hear something different. It lets each person enjoy it in his own way."

Ken said, "The man who wrote that good music sure did us a favor."

One day when the second grade went for music class, they told Mr. Danford, "Next week there'll be more of us than now—a whole class of visitors. Can we all do something together besides sing?"

Mr. Danford's first suggestion seemed so right that no other was needed. "You prepare paints, paper, and brushes. I'll prepare listening music. Each listener will use his paints and put on paper ideas that the music suggests. You and your friends will be surprised at the variety of the pictures that come."

"How did you know to think of it?" Laurie asked. "We've *never* painted to music."

The following week when the Japanese-American class and their teacher came, they brought two brand-new members, Kenji and Jiro. The two boys had arrived by air from Tokyo the previous afternoon. The fact that neither of them spoke or understood English did not fluster the welcoming committee. Laurie smiled at the newcomers and told them, "You understand music and painting and smiles. We do, too, so you'll be OK."

When the children took their places beside the paints and paper, Mr. Danford told them, "Some of you will get ideas quickly from the music. Others will want to listen for a while and then begin. Whenever the music's rhythm suggests a pattern and colors for your picture, pick up your brush and start. The music's suggestions will be different for each person."

The children's genuine interest in the resulting display —especially in the pictures of Kenji and Jiro—seemed proof enough that the communications system that day had been in excellent working order.

The class teacher told the children, "Your pictures tell us that you listened well to the music's message."

The visiting teacher said, "When we put our pictures on our classroom wall they will fill the room with music and make it a place where we want to be. You have made music become important to us in a new way."

Kenji and Jiro bowed, smiled, and said, "*Domo arigato Gozaimasu.*" Their teacher and classmates bowed, smiled, and said the same words. They explained that in English the words meant "Thank you very much."

Children in the third-grade classroom were not giving their customary good work, interest, and cooperation.

The teacher wondered, "Has my teaching suddenly become stunted and sparse? Or is the ground barren where it is falling?"

Then—the music teacher arrived. Conditions changed. Children changed. The classroom teacher changed.

The teacher at the piano directed the children, "Please push everything out of your hearing except the music I am playing. . . . Ready? . . . Let the flow of the music get inside you. . . . Feel the beat of the rhythm in your minds. . . . Now let some of the inside music come out. . . . In the air draw a picture of the beat. . . . Use large arm motions and make the picture large. . . . I want to see a picture of the inside music. . . . I see Lisa's. . . . I see Oscar's. . . . Good! . . . Good!"

Drawing a picture of music in the air caught the children's imaginations and challenged them immediately. "Give us another musical beat to draw in the air," they begged. "Two—three—a lot."

Now the music teacher said, "Those who want to may go to the chalkboard one at a time. There you will draw still another design as directed by the music. The music pattern will not change. It will be the same for each child. Listening, each child will create his own design as he feels it. No design will be like any other."

As each of the five designs emerged in turn from the same music pattern, those watching had five surprises. They watched Angelina's tall fence change in size. They watched Oscar's circle pattern get smaller and smaller as the music got softer and softer. When he had no more room for another circle, there was no more music. It had completely died away.

When Jean, who was last, finished her turn at the board, Lisa jumped from her chair. "Lets everybody make every design in the air. Angelina's first."

The repeated music pattern brought the children's arms into action. Already a child was asking, "Please may we do all of them again?"

Already the classroom teacher was thinking, "Oh, the joy in their faces! Each confident. Each realizing his own capacity to do in this new situation—to perceive things each time anew. In this experience they have been teaching me."

Jean's pattern

Joanne's pattern

John's pattern

Oscar's pattern

Angelina's pattern

A gift of music gives pleasure both to the giver and to the receiver. The gift of a song—words and music—went from one class to friends who could not see with their eyes that spring was on the way. Their song's words would remind of other ways that spring makes its coming known.

Oh, Welcome, Welcome, Springtime

Words and music by a second grade,
The Riverside Church.

1. Oh, wel - come, wel - come, Spring - time! The
2. How glad I am that Spring's begun! The

pit - ter pat - ter of the rain Falls
birds are sing - ing ev - ery - where, The

gent - ly on my win - dow - pane. I
flow - ers' fra - grance in the air, New

feel the warm rays of the sun And
grass is grow - ing at my feet, And

know that Spring - time has be - gun. Oh,
all the world smells fresh and sweet. Oh,

wel - come, wel - come, Spring - time!
wel - come, wel - come, Spring - time!

Another class sent their gift, a poem, to their friend, the carillonneur. For almost as many years as the children could remember, while playing in the park, skating on the sidewalks, riding along in a car, sitting near an open window in their apartment homes, they had heard tunes that floated down to them from the bells of the carillon.

Now, today, they had had the good fortune and privilege to sit with their friend inside the console booth high in the church tower. Saying not a word, making not a sound, they had watched his gloved clinched fists strike the many wooden handles of the keyboard, had watched his swift-moving feet manipulate the wooden pedals, sending out hymn tunes from big bells and little bells to be heard by passersby on the street, by worshipers in the church, and by themselves in the booth.

Back in the classroom Charlie said, "I won't forget him and how he makes music on the bells." Others added, "Me either." "Me either."

When their gift was written and ready to send, Marvin said, "Now maybe he won't forget us."

This is their poem. It holds ideas from each child in the class. All liked it. They called it their "ringing, swinging, singing poem."

> Bells! Bells!
> Ringing bells,
> Swinging bells,
> Singing bells.
> Ring out and swing out from your tower high.
> Sing out your music for all who pass by.
> Old songs and new songs,
> Sad songs and gay.
> Sing us your carols on glad Christmas Day.
> Sing of Thankgiving, and sing of our land.
> Music is something we all understand.

Ring out the Old Year,
Swing in the New.
Sing out to neighbors.
They're listening to *you!*

Singing is another way to enjoy music.

When the teacher spends time and uses imagination in preparation, the experience becomes one to anticipate. It is never commonplace or lacklustre. The music gates are open. Children sing at the worktable. They hum as they put on their coats.

One teacher shared with his class his interest in the *Bay Psalm Book,* the first book to be published (1640) in the American colonies. Stories of the period helped them remember events in the lives of these early settlers. They imagined how singing from this hymnal might, as Stewart said, "make their days go faster and be better." They recalled times in their own lives when singing changed a situation.

Jack, lonely on the first night at camp, joined to sing fun songs and shaking-hands songs around the campfire. On the way back to the tent he laughed with other boys and didn't feel one bit miserable anymore.

On Dora's first night on board ship everybody sang together in the big lounge. Next morning, walking on deck, people spoke to each other like friends.

Lois and her family camped at a national park. Each night the families sang together. It was nice.

Alma and her mother visited Alma's aunt in a strange city. They didn't feel strange at church. They knew the songs.

Another day, this teacher mentioned the musical instrument that each one of the children carried with him wherever he went. All were curious except Jack, who said, "My teacher at school told us about it. It's our voice and no two are ever exactly alike." At music time they listened to each other's instruments. Some were too loud. Some were too soft. Some you got tired of hearing. Some made you stop up your ears.

Iris said, "You have to make your instrument obey you. How it sounds is your responsibility."

Lynn told Mr. Wilson, the teacher, "Your instrument isn't bad at all."

In December Mr. Wilson introduced the carols he had searched for and found during the summer—carols enjoyed by children in different countries of the world. What better way than in song to capture the feelings of Christmas as children in other lands know them? Albert said, "Now that we sing the songs, they tie us to all the other children who sing them."

For this teacher, untrained in music, these satisfying touches with music provided the confidence needed to venture into others.

The making of simple musical instruments and using them purposefully can provide many hours of musical pleasure for children of all ages.

For one group of older children the making of instruments followed Alfred's discovery in a room that was long familiar. "Look!" he suddenly called one morning, pointing to the very top of one of the six tall plain glass windows, "A little colored window with pictures. Each window has one."

The children gathered around, stood on tiptoe and looked. None of them had ever noticed before what they now saw.

"There's a horn, or maybe its a trumpet."

"I see some cymbals."

"All the windows show musical instruments. Why?"

The teacher knew the answer. "The bright pictures in the medallion windows illustrate a praise song that was first sung long, long ago by the ancient Hebrews. This song is in our Bible. You may read it for yourselves."

In subsequent sessions the children read and reread the psalm. They also arranged its lines for choral reading and made, in ways that pleased them, instruments representing those mentioned in the psalm and discovered in the windows. Peggy explained, "Ours are for effect; they don't really make music."

From foil pans and streamers of narrow colored paper they created the cymbals. From cardboard, string, and gilt paint they created the harps and other stringed instruments. Trumpets and other wind instruments they made from paper and added painted decorations.

The psalm became part of a music service, some of the class reading the words as arranged, others using the instruments in rhythmical patterns developed to match the rhythm of the spoken words.

A music service in which the children played actual instruments for the enjoyment of the listeners was motivated by Jonathan's request, "May I bring my violin and play it for the first grade? My brother and his friends want to hear it." If one child wanted to share his music, others must have the same desire. The teachers felt remiss not to have thought of this practical and delightful idea themselves, not to have done something about it long ago.

The results of the first music service for all the classes warranted a second service the following year. The next year saw the service become an established custom. Each child who had music to share was invited to share it. The music supervisor listened to each selection a week or so prior to the service. In this way the timing of the various numbers could be estimated and the time of the service be kept within the half hour. A three-page piano selection could be shortened to one page, a three-stanza song to one stanza. One year, the instruments heard were the accordion, violin, flutophone, piano, and recorder. Two brothers sang, their mother being the accompanist. Two sisters played a duet. A brother and sister played a piano-violin duet. The contribution of a first-grade boy playing on the piano with one finger the tune of "America" was appreciated as much as that of a third-grade boy playing a difficult violin selection. An older girl whispered to her teacher, "It is a simple tune, but isn't he having a good time playing it?" Just how great his enjoyment was everyone knew when, at the close, eyes shining, he announced for all to hear: "I can play the second verse too!"

One year David's family participated with him—his father at the piano, his mother at the cello, his sister with her violin, and David playing the recorder.

Another year, upon entering the room, the children saw oversized notes made from colored paper arranged hit-and-miss fashion across a dark curtain at the back of the low platform. The service began with the story of a shepherd boy, David, who shared his music with a king, who was ill.

Another appealing element of music for children is its ability to enter into their mood and to follow it and conform to it as each one imaginatively becomes another person and interprets that person's actions through appropriate rhythmical motions. This use of music is described in the chapter "Informal Dramatics."

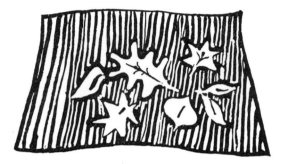

Pictures

"Look everybody . . .
Paul's made a picture . . .
A picture in the window!"

Laura, age 7

That morning in their classroom, the children quickly responded to Laura's summons, "Look!" The picture they saw was one not made with paints and paper. No! It was made with branches of red berries that Paul had brought from his own yard in New Jersey and a squat brown bowl that he had found on the classroom shelf. The wide windowsill must have beckoned, "I'm the just-right place for what you have made," for there is where Paul placed his picture. The children, reaching out and touching the bowl with its pretty berries, approved.

Wherever imagination is expected from children, wherever it is encouraged and accepted, children's pictures may be depended on to take many forms, to utilize unusual materials, and to be displayed in appropriate, if sometimes unconventional, places. Together, they guarantee a classroom environment that is lively and vital—proof positive to all who enter, "This room belongs to us."

Visitors to such a room seldom need the spoken word to catch an artist's mood, to understand the message that his picture tells, and to learn from it. With his picture, each artist announces, "Here is something that has happened to me. I am sharing it with you."

Some pictures record personal adventures. Some tell of trips, holiday parties, guests that the class has enjoyed. Others bring faraway story places within reach of the viewer's eyes. Still others make story people seem real. Bright designs also call out a message: "See what fun I've had with color." Whatever its theme, whatever its manner of development, each picture keeps alive in the artist's mind some memory of the past.

Sometimes one child's work and his attitude toward it gives an impetus, a sort of push, to another. A boy who has consistently said, "I can't think of anything to make," becomes absorbed in the giant-sized fish painted by his friend. Next week he digs deep within his own memory and discovers how mistaken he has been. The dog he fashions from clay brings praise from the whole class.

A girl who consistently dawdles now changes her pace with surprising results. This time, her work, not that of her friend, is finished first, is first to be displayed, and in the place of her choice.

A boy too often absent watches another add a red sail to the toy boat he is making. That very morning he tries the scroll saw and sandpaper. Soon his request startles the teacher: "I guess right now you already can mark me present for next week. My boat's got to get finished on time." Not long afterward children in a migrant camp play center are sailing many boats in large tubs of water. Their teacher's good news that day is: "The boats are your very own. They were made especially for you."

In certain classrooms, first-time visitors are sometimes astonished to discover that the ceiling becomes more than a covering overhead. Pictures hang from it! One ceiling decoration, a mobile of suspended balls of varying sizes, represents the solar system as fashioned by children. Another, of suspended papier-mache forms, illustrates the evolution of man.

A first grade's mobile tells of Thanksgiving. Using plastic coffee-can tops for paper and felt-tip markers for paints, the children have pictured the bountiful harvest. A red apple in this circle, purple grapes in that one, a yellow squash in another. Now the bright circular pictures hang at different lengths from a frame of crossed wires suspended from the ceiling. When a current of air touches them, they move. They twist. They turn. They are a pretty sight to see.

Visitors discover, too, that classroom floors are more than a place to walk, more than a place for furniture. Pictures are there! Lines of white tempera paint across one linoleum-covered floor picture the imagined size of a vegetable garden growing in the corner of a schoolyard in West Germany.

"Why this?" a visitor wants to know. The children tell her.

"Our money's what started it."

"We've got a stake in it."

"I counted all the seed packages and helped wrap the box to get mailed."

"I carried the box to the post office."

"I counted out the money we needed for postage."

The letter acknowledging their gift gave the children no picture, no outward vision of what the actual garden was like. They neither expected nor required it. Already they had visualized the distant garden in their minds and had made the size as they imagined it to be.

Their teacher told the visitor, "Had I encouraged them at any time to work from an outside model, copying it exactly as their eyes saw it, this would have been the equivalent of telling them, 'Your own precious gift of imagination is not important. Let it atrophy and wither away.' "

In the following weeks this class often walked in their garden. Here they became in story play the faraway children planting their seeds and tending them, gathering the ripened vegetables, cooking, eating, and enjoying them.

On another floor, there stood an Indian tepee made by the children. To them it seemed like a picture, too, with painted-on designs of the sun, moon, and stars. Inside the tepee, children welcomed each other with the Indian sign of greeting. They shared with the day's visitor the words of an Indian child's prayer, words that, in time, became their own:

> Great Spirit, send the light down on me today.
> Speed my good arrows swift on their way.
> Make my hands swift and my feet strong,
> Following the Great Trail all the day long.
> Lend me the Wind's breath, and the Sun's desire,
> And let the Moon lead me home to the tepee's fire.

Together, they considered where and how *their* "good arrows" might fall, the needed work *their* "swift hands" might do.

A first-grade teacher's India-print cotton spread became a picture on the floor when she placed it there for story-listening time. Its designs shimmered in the sunlight, red, blue, yellow, green, orange. The children hurried to take their places on it.

In classrooms that are the children's own, walls often are more than partitions dividing one part of the building from another. Pictures are there! What variety!

One wall picture that grew week by week extended to the north, south, east, and west of the large paper that bore its printed title "Our Map About Churches." Lines roughly sketched across the paper indicated five continents and the Atlantic and Pacific oceans. Many designs! Many ideas! Many artists at work! The result: an unusual pictorial map of real churches and churches that for the children existed only in stories.

Some of the children, in their eagerness to complete a design, were content to paint only the front view of the church, then, having cut it out, to paste it in place flat against the map. Others, more painstaking, folded their painted and cut-out pictures to be three dimensional, then thumbtacked them into place to extend out from the paper.

The church in Lapland was a reminder of Somi, the real boy who helped to build it. Monezip, a story friend, pictured beside her church in Africa, held the Bible she had bought for it by raising and selling peanuts. Children in Kansas, the class's favorite correspondents of the year, sent a we-made-it-ourselves picture of their rural church. Joost's picture showed the chapel of an ocean liner, which was his church while traveling back to Holland for a visit. Lucy's scene beside a lake in Maine represented her church during three weeks at camp. New York's Church of All Nations was on the map, too, its roof-playground and friends made there were long remembered.

Class visitors left their pictured signatures in place on the map, their drawings of home churches in Seattle, Rio de Janeiro, Albany, Houston, and other towns and cities.

"Think of it," the children said. "Outside, all different. Inside, all alike."

One teacher's contagious interest in news stories that picture people helping each other in unusual ways began another wall display. Soon the children were searching magazines and newspapers at home. What they found there kept the displays ever new, ever interesting. Picture news of:

Alaska's governor reading a small boy's letter which said, "Please use this money from my allowance to move all the people to a safe place where they won't have any more earthquakes."

A group of children, members of a neighborhood center in their crowded city, having their first fun with creative dramatics. Their club leader had retold their requested story and now the story people had come to life: Jack, Jack's mother, their cow, the Giant, and the Giant's wife.

A navy pilot landing his helicopter in New York's Central Park, while attendants from the hospital across the avenue stood ready with a stretcher to carry the fourteen-year-old passenger, ill with gas gangrene, to the medical specialists and their life-saving equipment.

On another classroom wall Emily and her father showed photographic slides of their family's trip by car across the United States. To the children, many of the slides seemed to be illustrations of a song they knew—spacious skies, fields of grain, majestic mountains, and the flat, level plains extending as far as eyes could see.

On still another wall, the children were surprised to find that such simple ingredients—a piece of old, freshly laundered sheet, a spray gun from the hardware store, and paints—could create such a pretty picture. On the cloth, they had pinned some ferns and leaves of different shapes. Over all of these they had sprayed tempera paint. Then, after removing the pins and discarding the ferns and leaves, they found an unusual picture.

"On the wall it looks like a real picture," commented one boy.

"It's a neat way to remember that good walk when we collected the ferns and leaves," commented another.

The teacher said, "Each one of you has other pictures stored in your minds from other good walks. Recall one that you would like to show us, but instead of using cloth and paints, show this picture to us in words. Think about this picture for a while, then let us see it, too."

The word pictures, with the teacher's help, were later put into rhyming lines and the result placed beside the cloth-and-paint picture.

> The house in Alice's picture, the one she made us see
> Was yellow, with eight singing birds up in her apple tree.
> With Dave we saw a small red light against the night's dark sky,
> Shining from his tall church tower, so bright and clear and high.

Then Jack we saw in his canoe, a-paddling on the lake.
Then Jane, who with her mother's help, did make and bake
a cake.

Dick took us to his grandma's yard the day that spring
broke out,
Peach trees in bloom and violets and jonquils all about.

Sue let us see her twenty trees all standing in a row
And in-between, bright sunflowers, all smiling, nodding so.

With Gail we picnicked at the beach, umbrellas in the
sand,
And watched the white-edged waves come dancing on
the land.

Past woodsy coves along the shore where pirates used to
hide
Chugged Pete's old-fashioned riverboat, a wheel upon
each side.
Then at the dock Pete threw out ropes, and soon the boat
was tied.

We also saw Ed's hurricane make branches break and
bend,
And watched the sunset from Dan's porch, all red and
gold. The end.

Visitors to an active and interesting classroom observe
that doors are more than movable wooden barriers that
turn on hinges for opening and closing the passageway between rooms. Pictures are there! One door picture is
made on yellow burlap, each of its sixteen designs, created
from bright yarn, felt, and metallic paper, represents a
church symbol.

Another, placed along seldom used folding doors, displays the entire first grade in life-size shapes cut from
paper. Placed side by side, as if holding hands, the jaunty
cut-out children seem to announce, "We're growing.
Measure how tall we are."

The door that his pupils push open at session's end

when leaving the classroom becomes for that teacher a place for reminder pictures. Each closing time finds the reminder message there to be read and, hopefully, remembered.

$5 69
Money Still Needed
to buy
Electric Saw
for the children at the
neighborhood center

Pictures teach in many ways. The imagination of the teacher determines how many, or how few.

Poetry

"The way the poem talks about snow, inside *of me I* feel that way, too. Only, outside *of me I can't think to* say the words myself."

Terrell, age 8

Ribbons of Rhyme [1]

Children,
Who showed you the path
Of the poets?

Who gave you the poet's purse
Jingling with coins of song?

In your seashell
You carry the shape of the sea.

[1] By Ryah Tumarkin Goodman, from *Horn Book* magazine, August 1967. Used by permission of Mrs. Goodman and the publisher.

Your hands hold
Echoes of waves.

Children,
Who twined ribbons of rhyme
In your hair?

Who showed you the path
Of the poets?

Happy is the teacher who has daily proof of his pupils' enjoyment of poetry. Then, daily he sings of his gladness," 'Twas I! Yes, I, who showed them the path of the poets. I, who twined ribbons of rhyme in their hair." Singing, he knows that on many tomorrows he again will share with the children the rhythmical, colorful words of the poet.

Tomorrow they will hear in those words the stillness of snow in the fields, waves of the ocean dashing against shores, the woodman's saw cutting trees in great forests, though snow, ocean, and woodman be a thousand and more miles away.

Tomorrow they will see in them, as if with their own eyes, the grace of the batter swinging to connect with the ball, of the ballerina dancing across the stage, of the procession marching row after row along the avenue, hands swinging, feet stepping, all in unison as if only one man marched to the music of the band.

Whatever the season, the poet's words can bring to the children many surprises—the fragrance of cherry blossoms in a Japanese garden, of pine trees atop a New England hill, of wild honeysuckle beside a Swiss lake. And many delights—the remembered taste of pumpkin pie at Thanksgiving, of popcorn balls at Christmas, of heart-shaped cookies on Valentine Day.

And let them feel, with a small boy, the fun of buying

a new pair of shoes; with a traveler, the loneliness of the deserted road on which he walks; with friends, the pleasure of the friendship shared between them.

Magic and music always await on the poet's path. Else how do children traveling there hear, see, smell, taste, and feel faraway experiences that seem real enough to be their own? How do they find thoughts there that give new meaning to all that they do? No ordinary passerby could work such magic for them, could offer such treasures.

This magic and music long have been part of man's life. No one knows who first thought of expressing thoughts in rhyming, singing words or who the first listeners were. But from earliest times, poets have wanted their listeners to remember their words, to feel the importance of the message the words bring, to be excited about it.

Yet those early poets, even as those today, often cleverly concealed a part of their message within their words. All of its meaning was seldom grasped immediately. Even after many listenings some bit still escaped.

When the ancient psalmist sang out his message:

The heavens are telling the glory of God;
Day to day . . .
    and night to night. . . .
There is no speech, nor are there words;
    their voice is not heard;
yet their voice goes out through all the earth,
    and their words to the end of the world.

some listeners must have pondered earnestly about it. Possibly they questioned each other.

"Is he saying that a voice that no person hears can go out through all the world?"

"I do not know. Can it be that some strange magic
that we do not understand makes words that are
not yet spoken travel to the end of the world?"

"His words seem only the simple words of a song. If
they bring a message why are we unable to understand it?"

Then they have gone on their way, never understanding its
meaning.

Others who heard may have drawn nearer and im-
plored:

"Sing your words once again. This time in livelier
fashion."

"Now let us hear them once more. Intone the words
slowly, slowly. Though your words be simple, we
want to possess the message that they bring, to
think about it day after day for all time."

Beginning at last to understand, they must have gone
on their way rejoicing in the wonder of its truth.

When today's readers of Chaucer first meet the strange
group of men and women journeying to Canterbury and
attempt to define the true character of any one of them,
are they successful? Who among them immediately recog-
nizes all that Chaucer tells concerning the virtues and
vices of any one of the diverse characters presented in
any of the tales?

Only scholars who have spent years, even a lifetime,
in the study of fourteenth-century life in London, who
understand how historical events, court customs, re-
ligious beliefs of that period affected the lives of rulers,
clergy, and common people of England, could begin to

speak with authority about any traveler or about the tale he told.

For centuries great men have considered poetry to be an essential part of the greatness of life, not an ornament added to an hour because nothing else was available.

To Alexander the Great, poetry was so essential that while on his conquests he carried with him, in a golden box, a copy of the *Iliad*. To James Wolfe, the English general, it was so important that on the eve of his victory over Montcalm, he told his council, "I would rather be the author of 'Elegy Written in a Country Churchyard' than to capture Quebec."

Whether the poet speaks across three hundred years, thirty years, or three years, he takes the reader on a journey. He brings him face to face with ideas. The reader— or listener—in his turn then invites those ideas into his mind so that he may become acquainted with them, a process that takes time. Possibly it never ends, for after a number of years of partial acquaintance with the ideas, a chance hour spent with them on another day may bring that flash of understanding of the once-elusive line, that sudden insight into the meaning of the once-difficult phrase. With the new understandings, the smaller ideas within the larger idea fall into place. The old acquaintance with the particular selection takes on new dimensions and begins afresh.

In every period of time the poet has much to say. He looks into human hearts and describes what he finds there with a vividness that lets the listener also feel the reality of what he finds; with an insight that gives him a deeper self-understanding; with a rhythm that sends him off to a daily life of good will among neighbors near and far; with a beauty of language that inspires him to observe close-at-hand wonders that too often he leaves unnoticed;

with a wisdom that permits a deeper appreciation of the mystery and majesty of the universe of which he is a living, breathing part.

The teacher, then, eager to enrich the lives of his pupils with the treasured findings of the poet, seeks first to enrich his own life with them. He earnestly searches for poems in which he may discover for himself vividness, insight, rhythm, beauty, and wisdom.

The search takes time. Like the journey, it is continuous. It reaches here, there, and has no end. The teacher, confident that there is a poem for every need, is willing to search until he finds it. For him, poetry is a *must* tool for his teaching.

Finding the poems, those he is certain to use and those he will have ready just in case, he makes their acquaintance. Some he stores in his memory, to be called on at will. Others he copies on the pages of his always-in-reach notebook. All eventually become a part of him. It matters not when the moment of sharing comes, he is prepared then to open the poem's door and to introduce the children to what is inside.

For one class the looking inside came following Jerry's recounting of a recent—and first—ride on the merry-go-round. Taking Jerry's hand, the teacher invited the children, "Come! Find a partner. Let's all ride with Jerry on the merry-go-round."

Following the leaders, the children, two by two, circled the room on their pretend horses, moving in unison to the rhythm of the just-in-case rhymed lines which the teacher repeated and which the "riders" quickly learned and repeated with her.

> Together astride our two fine white steeds,
> Trotting around in incredible speeds,

We ride, we two, to the rollicking sound
Of the merry, merry tune
Of the merry-go-round.

The poetry-using teacher's ever ready notebook is large. It holds the poems now in use and those that will be used in the future. Its blank pages await those yet to be found. Each collection represents the choices of the individual who collects them. No two are identical. Each, however, probably will include groups of poems that speak on the same topic, as, for example, games, favorite toys, children's growth. Also there will be poems that relate to holidays, birthdays, the weather, the seasons, and similar occasions that are certain to appear within each year.

In addition, the teacher of younger children probably will include in his collection poems about animals, fun at work and play, trips, friends near and far. The teacher of older children will include those that tell a story, present some of the mysteries of the world, bring views of real people and real places around the world, take the listeners on adventures under the seas and into outer space.

In presenting poetry to children, the wise teacher remembers that children seldom like poems that preach, are too long, have too much description and too little action, use figures of speech; that children's ears usually are atune to repetitive phrases, to lively rhyming schemes both in words and in matching lines, to word pictures that describe the familiar.

He remembers also that the person presenting the poem to children does not:

Explain its message. The poet does not need such help. His own tools—rhythm, rhyme, color—are quite adequate to make the meaning clear.

105

Give the poet's biographical data. The children's interest centers upon what the poem's words say to them, not in where and when the poet was born.

Discuss its rhyming pattern. To do so contributes nothing to the listeners' understanding of the words.

Paraphrase its lines. When he does this, the carefully designed word pictures, the rhymes, the meter, the mood, all are lost.

Use an elocutionary style, voice trembling, arms gesturing. The poet asks only that the reader act as the medium by which the mood of the poem, its ideas and feelings, may touch the listener.

Expect the children always to see, understand, and enjoy the pictured words of the poem after hearing them only once. These results come after much sampling, much time.

Expect the children always to enjoy it after their own silent reading of it. In such a reading they miss the galloping, skipping, marching movements of the words which are detected only when lifted from the printed page and spoken aloud.

Expect to have immediate success with every poem he shares. Practice in reading it is essential. Also essential are his own enjoyment and understanding of it. A glance at his listeners brings to the reader their verdict of how he is doing.

Suggest, "Let's all memorize these lines for tomorrow." When the child desires to learn a favorite couplet or longer verse he will do so of his own volition. He needs no suggestion from another.

In introducing poetry to children, the teacher starts where the children are, with poems that they understand. Perhaps he tells them, "A first-time reading of a poem is something like opening a surprise package. You look at the outside of it. You untie it. You lift out the surprise." They may believe, he tells them, that the idea they lift out of the poem is the only one there. But after reading the poem or listening to it a second time, a third time, they just might discover another idea there, or perhaps two. Like a set of nested boxes, each box fitting cozily within another, the smaller ideas fit neatly into the larger one, are related to it, and are a part of its design. To enjoy poetry, he says, the children must not be content with merely discovering the original surprise; they must find the hidden ones, too.

After interest is aroused, the teacher moves slowly, guiding each child into areas of reading where his particular interests lie, always encouraging, always ready to offer specific help, if needed.

"You will like this poem. One of its ideas relates to an important event in American history."

"After reading this poem I said, 'This is for Lucien.' So here it is. After you find its message you'll know why I called it your poem."

"You like short poems. To present so many pictures of a fog in so few words is not easy. Why not try it yourself?"

The child who enjoys poetry grows with it. His interest can lead in many directions. Like children in Korea he may join his family in creating poems about happy shared experiences, a walk in the woods in spring, the visit of a friend.

Like children in Holland, he may add to the fun of Saint Nicholas Day by creating a rhymed verse for each member of the family that contains clues about where each must look if he is to find his hidden gift.

Like children in Sweden he may use red ribbon and tie to each gift that he has chosen for others a rhyme containing clues about the identity of the gift. Before opening the package each person reads his verse aloud and all take turns guessing what might be inside.

Or, like no one except himself, he may surprise Father with a birthday verse created especially for him, or seven poems, one for each day that friend Joey will be in the hospital.

In time, these same children will be reading good poetry of their own choosing, will be buying books of poetry with their own money, will be discovering that poetry gives an additional pleasure and richness to their lives. In time, perhaps, also creating worthy poems of their own to be shared with children on the poet's path.

Peter's teacher helped him find that path. To do this for his pupils is the privilege of every teacher.

Poems[2]

In poems, our earth's wonders
Are windowed through
   Winds.

A good poem must haunt the heart
And be heeded by the head of the
   Hearer.

With a wave of words, a poet can
Change his feelings into cool, magical, mysterious
   Mirages.

Without poetry our world would be
Locked within itself—no longer enchanted by
   the poet's Spell.

[2] Peter Kelso, age eleven, Australia, in *Miracles,* Richard Lewis, ed. Copyright © 1966 by Richard Lewis and reprinted by permission of Simon and Schuster.

Writing

"You know what? If you take a pencil along and write down what we tell you when we're inside the sukkah, we won't have to stay busy keeping so much in our heads while we're seeing everything. When we come back then we'll write the story and nothing will get left out."

Bradford, age 7 1/2

Creative writing never just happens. No! It comes when the right ingredients are put together in the right way—a child . . . an experience . . . special words with which to describe the experience . . . an atmosphere that encourages the expression of ideas about the experience . . . a teacher, parent, friend who listens well, who has faith, patience, an honest interest, a pencil in readiness.

The experience may come at any time, at any place. When it comes during a school session it may be the result of some part of that day's teaching—a story, poem, filmstrip, music, a visitor, a trip, something seen from the window. It may come from the child's own feelings —anger, curiosity, friendliness.

When the experience touches the child significantly, he not only gives back what he has taken in, but also adds his own thoughts and impressions. It is this added bit of his own personality that gives the experience its distinction, its greatest worth.

Sessions that are dull, repetitive, predictable, with no surprises, no added contraband, seldom produce topics for writing or children who want to write. They bring no air of excitement, no happy chattering, no bubbling over.

Teachers who believe in children, who see creative writing not as a task to be over and done with as soon as possible, but as a means of helping children grow, are quick to provide the surprises, the contraband, to await the excitement. They enjoy the children. They listen to their ideas and show enthusiasm about those ideas.

Inside and outside the classroom they initiate experiences which encourage the children to observe and feel, to wonder and question, to think and understand. Then, if their first attempts at guiding the children's writing do not reach their own high expectations, they conceal their disappointment and keep trying. Success, they realize, cannot be guaranteed on any particular day, but it will come. Give up? Never.

Once properly motivated, the children, whether as individuals or a group, write more easily. To them there is no problem about an opening sentence, the logical progression of events, a clever ending. They remember what was important to them, and they have the vocabulary needed to describe it.

They begin. "Today we went to see a new baby and his name is Douglas. . . ."

They continue. "He's cute, but he can't do very much. . . ."

They stop. "We're making him a toy."

Children's writing comes when the children wish it to come, not at the signal of a gong or the urging of a teacher. In time they discover that what they write brings enjoyment to others besides themselves.

> A visitor asks for a copy of their snow song: "You describe the beauty and wonder of snowflakes in ways I never could have thought of myself."

> Duncan's grandfather writes from Minnesota: "The story your class wrote about your imaginary trip to the boys' school in India took your grandmother and me there, too. We have enjoyed our trip and have learned new information about the country and the people. Thank you, and please let us travel with you again."

They discover, too, that what they write they can re-read and relive tomorrow, next year, or in fifty years! There it is, spread out on the pages, waiting.

The expectant teacher and his ready pencil make possible such rereading and reliving of experiences enjoyed in the past. Without them, the descriptive phrase, the imaginative expression, the colorful conversation are never captured in their exactness and entirety.

When the first grade went walking in a nearby park one autumn day, the teacher followed along beside one child then another, enjoying their enjoyment of the scene around them. Some of the children chattered to themselves as if telling themselves a story, a little now, more later. Listening and writing, this teacher captured the following, in fragments, from Ned:

> Falling, falling leaves
> Fluttering, fluttering leaves
>   Red and yellow,
>   Purple, brown.
> The wind blows the leaves
> Scuffle, scuffle,
> Through the trees.
>   When winter comes
>   You sleep, sleep, sleep.
>   Snow covers you
>   Like a blanket.

And this from Virginia:

> Squirrels, squirrels
>   Gathering nuts
>   Going with them up the trees
> In they put them,
> In the holes.
>
> Down they scamper to the ground.
> Off they go to get some more.
> Squirrels, squirrels
>   Gathering nuts.

Other teachers found poems waiting to be expressed following the viewing of a film. How attentive the children. How exciting and true the story—birds returning in the spring to Northern homes after long months in warm South lands. Across sea and land, mountains and valleys they came, thousands of miles, each coming back to the home he had left so long ago, to the same farm, to the same barn on the farm, to the same rafter in the barn.

"How do they do it?" the first grade wondered.

"Have they got built-in compasses?"

"But what tells them when to start?"

"And how to go exactly where they want to go?"

Ken said, "How do they even know how to fly? Birds fly high in the sky. But when I try, I can't fly. Not even one inch. Why?"

The teacher, attentive and listening, heard the rhythm and the rhyme. "Ken, your words *sound* like a poem. Let's print them on the board and see if they *look* like a poem."

Birds
 fly
  high
In the sky.

But
 when
  I
   try,
I can't fly.

Not
 even
  one
   inch!
Why?

Ken was pleased. After he and the other children had looked at and read the printed words, he told the teacher, "My mother sure will be surprised that I made a poem."

Second-grade Edith also spoke about the wonder and mystery of the birds' long flight by day and by night back to the place where they had lived so many months ago:

> I don't know how God makes so many birds.
> They look like airplanes when they fly.

So swift, so quick they plan,
And fly together through the sky.

"Maybe he'll come out today." The children were hoping it out loud as they gathered around a glass box in place on the classroom table. The box was special. Inside there were several kinds of twigs. On one pine twig there was a small, small house. Inside the small house, a small creature was almost ready to emerge.

Watching and waiting, the children talked to him. The captured parts of their conversation also looked like a poem when the teacher put them together and printed them on a large sheet of paper.

> Little spider, tiny spider,
> Come out of your winter home.
> Crawl down the pine bough
> And spin us a web
>   In a pretty design,
>   Fine
>   Like lace.
>
> To see you, to watch you
> Will make us happy.
> Will make us gay.
> Will make us want to sing.
>   Little spider, tiny spider,
>   Sign of Spring.

In Craig's third grade, the inspiration for writing came from Craig himself. On that morning he shared with the class something that he had clipped from the newspaper that week—the President's Thanksgiving Proclamation.

"Why can't we make a proclamation?" he proposed.

No one seemed particularly enthusiastic, yet no one offered objections. There were questions. What will we proclaim? To whom? Why? When? How?

When the lively exchange of words seemed to be getting nowhere, Larry gave it a direction: "Let Craig read the proclamation one more time. Then everybody cut out talking and begin thinking."

As the thinking progressed, so did the plan. The proclamation would be addressed to children of the second, third, and fourth grades because they needed to be reminded of their good country, of the people who started it, of their own responsibility to keep it a good country. On the Sunday before Thanksgiving, copies of the proclamation would be given to each class. It would help them to remember the importance of its message even after Thanksgiving Day had passed.

The ideas to be proclaimed were listed on the board as individual children offered them. When the number seemed exhausted, they began to arrange the lines. Phrases were shifted here and there, then back again, until each seemed to be in the right place. Sometimes another word was substituted for the one given earlier and tried. If better, it was kept. If not, the original was restored. The children worked to think of words that let the listener *see* the message as well as *hear* it. Finally, the lines were read aloud in choral fashion and changes made to improve the rhythm.

A Proclamation

To all you children of this church:
Listen!
Give thanks!
Be glad!

Be glad for this land that is your home.
Grassy hills and snowy mountains.
Shady trees and fragrant flowers.

115

Be glad because you are a part of this land,
    America.

Give thanks for sun and rain, day and night.
For each season as it comes.
Planting time and harvest time.
Fruits, vegetables, all your food.
Be glad because the good gifts of this land are
    yours to enjoy.

Give thanks for people.
Indians, who taught the white man in many ways,
Leaders today, who make the laws of the land.
Doctors, teachers, parents, children,
All who make this land a good land,
All who work to keep it so.
Be glad that you, too, are a person.
That you, too, can do good
    and bring gladness wherever you go.

Listen, all you children of this church.
Give thanks!
Be glad!

A visit to the *sukkah* was an experience that filled the children with a new discovery, that gave them much to say, that made them eager to say it in writing.

That week the colorful booth had been built in the neighborhood, in the courtyard of the Jewish Seminary of America. In preceding weeks the class had prepared for the visit. They listened to stories of the ancient people who lived as nomads in the desert, wandering from place to place and dwelling in tents; of farmers of Palestine who erected small booths in their fields and vineyards during the harvest season and slept in them, guarding their crops from thieves and wild animals.

They learned some of the ancient laws of sharing. They read for themselves the law given to those long-ago people by God through Moses: "Go out to the hills and bring branches of olive, wild olive, myrtle, palm, and other leafy trees to make booths."

They prepared a list of questions to ask Mr. Remer, the student at the seminary who would be their host for the visit. Then, approching the courtyard, they heard their teacher's reminder, "Enjoy the *sukkah* not only with your eyes, but with *all* your senses."

The story of the visit—a long story to which each child contributed—was shared with other classes at the Thanksgiving service. Karl told his teacher that day, "Everybody listened good to our story. I think they liked listening like we liked writing."

Every year, about in October, do you know what? A *sukkah* is built in our neighborhood. This year we saw it in the courtyard of the Jewish Seminary. Mr. Remer helped us. Now he is our friend.

The *sukkah* is a big tent, only you don't know it because green leafy branches cover all the walls inside and outside. They even reach across the opened-up top, and the sun shines down through them in the day, and the moon shines through in the night.

Standing by the tent door Mr. Remer told us that *Sukkos,* the Festival of Ingathering, is the happiest of all the Hebrew festivals, a time of gathering in the harvest and giving thanks to God for his goodness. He taught us the prayer each person says before going inside the booth, and we said it with him.

"We thank thee, O God, King of the Universe,
For all thy many blessings.
And for bringing us again
To the joy of this day."

Everything inside smelled good, like in the country. We looked and looked. How could they make it so pretty! Cornstalks were beside the door. Fruits and vegetables

more than you could believe, were hanging on all the
walls, mixed up with the branches:
 purple grapes and purple eggplants
 orange oranges and orange pumpkins
 yellow bananas and yellow squash
 red apples and red peppers
 strings of white popcorn and white turnips
 green pears and green cucumbers
 and a lot of others.

Tables with white cloths and bowls of flowers were
inside the tent. Friends were eating and talking together.
Mr. Remer said that some came from far Boston and Phila-
delphia, and some came from near Long Island and Brook-
lyn. We could tell this was a happy holiday. It felt like it.

Now we know that the Pilgrims in Massachusetts were
not the first people to give thanks for the harvest.
 Long before Jesus was born,
 long before Columbus discovered America,
 long before George VI was King of England,
 the ancient Hebrews built booths and thanked
 God for the good fruits and grain. And their
 grandchildren and theirs and theirs keep right on
 doing it to this very day.

When a child becomes excited about study materials
that help him to see some fragment of life in a new
light, he is almost certain to come face to face with a
topic that calls out to him, "Tell about this in *your* way,
as *you* see it, as *you* feel it." When this happened to
Neel, he chose writing as the means he would use.

Neel's real home was in Virginia. New York City became
the family's one-year home. In the fourth grade's social
studies in day school, Neel's interest was captured by
stories of the early Dutch settlement on Manhattan Island and the contrast between life on the island then
and now.

His rhymed appraisal begins:

New York is quite some little city
Although some say, "New York's a pity."
It's got no meadows, no rolling hills.
It's got no village green.
But what it's got is quite enough
To make it quite a scene.

It has no Lincoln, nor Jefferson.
It has no Washington.
But those it had were great enough
To make it Number One.

In church school, a fifth grade's interest was captured by the stories of Hebrew life in the time of Abraham. The material introduced many inviting topics for individual and group writing. In a letter signed by Mishya, a boy who might have lived in those long ago times, one group described the hardships of caravan travel as Mishya, his family, other families, and their animals wander in search of water:

. . . Two nights ago when the caravan stopped, I was very tired but could not rest. I must help put up the tent, to drive the stakes, stretch the ropes, unload the camels, spread out the rugs. Then milk the goats so the babies would stop their crying for milk.

I slept for a long time. Then felt my mother shaking me and crying out, "Wake up, lazy Mishya. We must travel on." A stone bruise was on my big toe. It hurt. I did not want to get up. But they took the tent down from over me. There I was, lying in the hot sunshine. I got up and ran after them. We marched all day. The way was rough, many rocks, one hill after another, the sun beating on my back. I wanted a drink, but my mother said, "Wait till evening."

That night I was hungry and thirsty, too. There was only a sip of water, a little cheese, and curds for each person. I ate mine quickly and rolled up in my goatskin coat and slept. And dreamed of good things to eat.

All that day I trudged through more sand, over more hills. I had blisters on my feet, and my tongue was swollen until it felt too big for my mouth. I felt like crying. But I knew better than to whine or complain.

Then my father, one of the scouts who had gone ahead, came running back along the caravan, calling, "Courage! Courage! Only a little farther. I have seen it. Beautiful blue water lying among the hills."

I ran. I forgot I was tired. I came to the green trees and grass. I dropped down to drink. Then I spat the water from my mouth. That beautiful water was bitter! So bitter, that though we were famished for it, we could not drink one drop. Everyone wept.

Then an old man called out, "I will show you. Take branches from this tree. Throw them into the water." We obeyed. Soon the water was sweet and good. We drank all we wanted. We filled all the waterskins. We watered the sheep and camels. We bound up our poor, blistered feet. Then it was growing dark and time to set up camp once more.

This is all I will tell you this time.

Your far away friend,
Mishya

Two seventh-grade boys came face to face with a problem that to them seemed current and up-to-date, only to discover that it had touched people's lives centuries ago.

The question, raised in class, was this: "Is it better for a person to depend on another individual to tell him which is the right action to take, or should he depend on himself to know which is right, which is wrong?"

In reply, the teacher told an episode from Samuel's life.

When the people begged Samuel, "Give us a leader! Give us a king!" Samuel told them, "I will give you a king, but it is better for you to understand what is right and to listen to a voice that is God, than for you to have a king to tell you what to do."

The class developed a service that expressed their understanding of Samuel's teaching. The two boys wrote the prayer that closed this service.

God,
We would like to be able to listen to an inner voice
as Samuel did.
We know that there is an inner voice which we must obey.
May we always be free of a dictator or of anybody
who tells us exactly what to do.
May we know what is right and do it because it is right.
Now, as always, there are many voices crying,
"Give us a king!" because it is easier to be told
what to do.
Help us to obey the inner law of right.

Holidays unlock memories.

When an entire class begins to share memories of "Last Christmas when I saw the ballet The Nutcracker," "The Christmas when I met Uncle John at Penn Station," "The Christmas when I painted all the wrapping paper for our presents and my mother didn't have to buy any," "The Christmas when my father had to cut off the Christmas tree to make it fit," their words become a kaleidoscope of bright, flashing pictures that bring new and different views of a season that all hold dear.

And when a teacher helps the children put those bright pictures into writing, the pictures can come flashing into minds at any season.

One teacher's question of only three words brought answers filled with pictures.

What is Christmas?
It's marketing and cooking,
Popping open the oven, looking!

It's families together again.
Brothers and sisters home from school,
Grandparents come to visit.
All belonging.
All enjoying.

It's a red bow on a package,
A holly wreath on the door.
Santa Claus in a store window,
And—oh—lots and lots more.

It's tall candles shining,
Choir voices bringing
The story of a Baby
Born long, long ago.

What is Christmas?
It's all of these together
Yet words cannot tell all of it.
Colors cannot paint all of it.
Music cannot sound all of it.

It's the glad feeling that's there
Deep down inside of you
Because a gift from far away
Has come to you with love
And you know the love
Has come to stay.

An angry outburst between two pupils was the motivation for another group's cooperative writing.

"What word best describes the start of what we have just seen and heard?" the teacher asked.

"Anger," chorused the children.

"Then let's stop a while and give some attention to this word," the teacher continued.

"Do we have to?" growled the two culprits.

"No, we don't have to. But it may help us see an old subject in a new way."

"I vote for talking," said a nonangry one. Others nodded their agreement. The class put the result of their discovery into writing. This and the two other examples which follow bear the group's distinctive mark and spark.

Anger and Love

Anger is many things.

It's . . .
  the sound of a frowning voice
  the feel of thick spiked shoes
  the growl of a wild animal
  the boiling feeling inside us
  the awful murders we see in the paper.

But love is even more things.

It's . . .

  someone's quiet voice
  the feeling we have when a good story ends
  the way your hands feel when they run over a smooth jar
  when you come close to your mother and she gives you a hug and kiss
  the way you want to run around—everywhere and nowhere—on a bright, sunny day.

There are lots of times when anger knows us.
But love is so much bigger.
It can get right inside us and—*shove*—out goes anger!

This class, along with their absorbed interest in the story of Anne Sullivan Macy, listened one day to the poem "Unseen" by Arthur Guiterman. In the poem, a blind child gives his description of what he imagines certain colors are like.

Ross wondered, "If I couldn't see, what would I think those colors are like?"

The teacher said, "Close your eyes. Imagine them for yourself."

Soon all were trying. Then, not to be influenced by the poem's words, they chose colors different from those the blind child described.

Colors

Black is . . .
>the feel of
>>mud squishing through your fingers and toes
>>fog sneaking in all around the city
>the sound of
>>a thunder cloud when it breaks open
>>a still night all around you
>>a wave crashing down on the shore
>>a hurricane
>the taste of
>>licorice
>>>charcoal
>>>>and burned toast . .
>>>>>that's black!

Orange is . . .
>the feel of
>>the hot, hot sun on your body when you're sun-
>>>burning
>the sound of
>>a fire crackling in the fireplace
>the smell and taste of
>>orange soda
>>>pumpkins
>>>>and oranges . . .
>>>>>that's orange!

Brown is . . .
    the feel of
      heavy rough paper
      the bark of an oak tree
    the sound of
     a bear when it growls
    the smell of
      horses and hair
    the taste of
      gingerbread men and chocolate
    the way a bumpy dirt road throws
                   dirt
                  in
                    your
                     eyes . . .
                       that's brown!

Another day, the class heard the first of a series of stories about Louis Braille. The chapter title "A Window Rises" caught their imagination. They summarized in writing their discussion of this phrase.

When we open a window many things come in . . .
    Wind
      Rain
        Sunlight
        Moonlight.
People have windows, too.
Eye windows
Mind windows
When we open these windows something wonderful
    comes in.
      Ideas!
Think of the ideas that come in through the mind windows
    of these men . . .
      Ideas for the touch alphabet—Louis Braille
      Ideas about exploring—Davy Crockett and Daniel
      Boone

Ideas for making milk pure—Louis Pasteur
Ideas about a vaccine for polio—Jonas Salk
Ideas about freedom for all men—Abraham Lincoln.

Think of the ways men have used their ideas . . .
Painting them to become pictures
Putting them into notes to become music
Putting them into words that dance and sing in poetry
Putting them into diagrams and plans to become
buildings and roads and bridges.

Do you know what we think?

God must have the *most* good ideas.
Think of the flowers
the trees
the animals
the people
the earth
the universe
the galaxies
and outer space.

And do you know what else we think?
Every time a window opens in somebody's mind,

God is there!

The teacher whose mind leaps ahead and sees possibilities within a class situation that go unnoticed by one unaccustomed to looking for them is often rewarded by valuable topics for writing. When some child later remarks, "What *we* thought of today was good, wasn't it?" he experiences one of teaching's greatest satisfactions.

A teacher like this tossed out some questions to the children as they made plans for guests coming from a church in a distant part of the city.

How do you suppose those children and their teachers will feel, coming to a strange place in a strange part of the city?

What does the word "welcome" mean?
How does one give it?
How does one feel about receiving it?
What does being a friend mean?
Where did you find your answer?
How can you be certain that the rules for friendliness
work the same on Wednesday as on Sunday?
In summer as well as in winter?
In Albany and Buffalo as well as in New York?
In the course of finding answers, the children wrote:

How can I be a friend?
Being one is not easy.

It means stopping thinking so much about yourself,
and beginning thinking more about somebody else.
It means seeing in your own mind ways to make
that person happy, then doing them.

Like sharing your toys and books with him.
Letting him play with your dog.
Giving him what you, yourself, want.
Helping him when he needs help.

It means *not* giving an "eye for an eye" like the old law
said.
But treating him as you would like to be treated.
Remembering that he is a person with feelings.
Remembering that it is not just for *one* day, but for
every day.
Not just for *one* place, but wherever you are.

Real friendliness never stops.
It goes on and on and on.
It depends on you.

A vacation-school teacher saw a learning situation in
the word "importance," found in the material planned for
that day's session. Certain questions and possible answers

passed through his mind. The questions he asked the children included:

What does the word "importance" mean?
How does one get it?
Does everybody have it?
Does everybody want it?
Is it good to have?
When a person has it, how does he feel?

The children's answers are found in the summary written by Anne, Robin, and Marita.

We talked about when we feel big.
We talked about when we feel small.
We thought of the atom to make us feel big.
We thought of the world to make us feel small.

How important are all things small?
Are things—or people—only important if tall?
An atom can be most important, though small.
When do we feel most important of all?

At Grand Central Station or any other station,
Nobody sees us and we feel very small.
Each person is hurrying. He might miss his train.
We don't exist to those people at all!

But it's different at home. There people love us.
Love is most important of all.
We don't see it or touch it or smell it or hear it.
But everyone who feels it knows he's important.
The old and the young, the tall and the small.

One teacher's first venture with writing came after the class had returned from a visit to nearby International House. Directives from a recently read book flashed an encouraging signal:

"Children value their own experiences as subjects for writing."

"A group experience lends itself to group dictation."

"We shall see," the teacher told himself, and made the plunge by suggesting to the children, "Instead of painting pictures to tell about our trip, let's write words to tell about it."

"You mean like a story?"

"Exactly. Each person will tell what he remembers best and what he liked best, and we'll put all the ideas together to make the story."

With the unexpected flow of contributions, another statement from the book came flashing: "Children's confidence in their writing often gives confidence to the teacher." Suddenly, the teacher's thought pattern changed from "Keep going, Mister Faint-Heart" to "Continue on, Mister Confidence."

With confidence he spoke out. "Tony called International House a 'world home.' What makes a place a home? Are your apartments and houses homes? Why? Some people call this building where we come each week a 'church home.' Why? If International House *is* a world home, what makes it one?"

While the teacher continued to write the children's comments as quickly as his brand of shorthand would permit, the children continued to talk and to watch the writing. They could hardly believe they had said so much —six pages full!

The teacher explained, "This part of story-writing is called 'gathering the data.' Some people believe it is the most important step in writing. Next week we'll organize the data, and the following week we'll begin the writing. If you have more ideas, fine. There will be a place for them."

The next week the children saw their story begin to take on pattern and form. Their many ideas fell into place in orderly fashion. The following week, when the writing was finished and the children read and reread their story, some of the boys said, "It takes too long to read." But no one could suggest even one line to take out, so nothing was changed.

You may live in a house,
Eat there, sleep there, use it for shelter,
But these do not make your house a home.
A house is empty until you add love.
A house + a family + fun + love = a home.

Houses have signs to tell you they are homes.
Inside, families make the signs.
Outside, passing neighbors hear them.
 "Thank you."
 "Please."
 "Sure. It's OK with me."
 "I'll help."
 "You're welcome."

You may see a building with colored glass windows,
With stone carvings and pretty lights,
Even a steeple on top and a ringing bell.
But these do not make the building a church home.
A building + the Bible + a minister who explains the
 Bible's words + people who care about other
 people + love = a church home.

Inside there are signs that tell you it's a church home.
 Music and singing and happy people.
 No one pulls everything to himself.
 He works to give other persons exactly what he enjoys
  for himself even if those persons live in countries
  across the ocean.

Near our church home there's a big stone building.
Words over its door say International House.
We know because we have been there.
Tony called it a "world home" because students from all
 over the world live there.

Inside this house also are a restaurant, gift shop, a post office, and barber shop.

But these do not make this house a world home.

The building + world students studying, working, playing, being friends, and finding ways to make each one glad that he came + love = a world home.

Inside we saw the signs.

By the front door, Miss Phillips from Ceylon welcomed us.

In a quiet room upstairs she answered the fourteen questions, which we had written on paper.

In the gym students from Brazil, Hawaii, Burma, and Canada played badminton.

In the music room students with light hair and dark hair, light skins and dark skins listened to records and invited us to listen, too.

In the reception hall students wearing saris, kimonos, bright skirts and blouses, and men in turbans talked to us.

In the home room there was a picture of Mrs. Edmonds, who had the idea to build this world home.

Family Home, Church Home, World Home,
When you know about them,
They are not very different.

Parents

"My father's got a box full of helping tools—hammers and saws and glue. He'll help us make the train."

Bill, age 8

Parents are people. People who hold within their memories and in the skills of their ten fingers riches that can give special dimension to any day's teaching. When these are brought into the classroom and shared with children and teacher, they:

> Make possible a richness of content and a variety of activities that the teacher could not accomplish alone.

> Add a kind of contraband that assures an extra dividend in that day's learning and enjoyment.

Give the participating parent a view of the study unit that he could gain in no other way.

Cause the children to say, "Please make the clock go slower. We don't want to go home yet."

Parents are people—busy people who, when they know the *what, when, why,* usually smile, say "Yes," and give generously of their skill, their time, and of themselves.

To one teacher it was obvious that Molly's mother was skillful with needle and thread. So she took the initiative. "Mrs. Kester, Molly and the other children in our class are becoming magicians! With bright yellow curtains of their own creation they plan to transform the dark class-room where they visited last week into one where the sun always will seem to be shining. Could you help thread needles and knot threads for twenty minutes during our next two sessions?"

Mrs. Kester could! Her neighbor came, too, as co-helper, and the resulting assembly line of workers found needles always threaded, threads always knotted, and no time lost.

Sometimes a child announces a parent's qualifications as a helper. "My father's got a box full of helping tools—a hammer and saws and glue. He'll help us make the train."

The teacher follows through. "Mister Bell, Bill has told us about that helping box of yours. The engine and caboose of the train the class is making for the kinder-garten at Neighborhood House could profit by the con-tents of that box if you will come with them. Could you, for the next two sessions? You decide the time."

A month later, with a hearty laugh, Mr. Bell explains the reason for his double overtime work periods. "I had to make certain that the boys had the headlight in place, the flag flying at the rear of the caboose, and all the cars in good pulling condition."

Sometimes the child is so proud of a parent's talents that he commits the parent to an assignment without his knowledge.

Phyllis' class, through the Community Service Society, had arranged to play *The Three Kings* to a family recently arrived from Puerto Rico, the father being ill. One morning, while working on the small gifts they were making for each member of the family, Dwight's idea popped out in words.

"If we put a new five-dollar bill in an envelope, extra, then the mother can buy special food for dinner on Three Kings Day. And all the family will get some benefit."

Phyllis, usually not so quickly agreeable to another's idea, beamed her approval. "My mother crochets the *prettiest* pocketbooks. She'll make us one to hold the money."

Phyllis' mother, when approached by the teacher, exclaimed in dismay, "This on top of everything else! And Christmas practically here. I don't see how I . . ." Then a quick smile. "But of course I can. I'd forgotten that Three Kings Day is not until January. If Phyllis thinks the money should be in a pretty pocketbook instead of a paper envelope, then it will be."

Later, seeing the bill in its elegant container, Dwight announced, "In there it sure looks like more than five dollars."

Judy's father also obliged when Judy, without asking, committed his services to the class. The children had listened to the story of seven-year-old Kotuka, who did not like school. School had no wonders, only desks and books. Every day he wanted to stay in his garden. Many wonders were there: a rabbit, grass, flowers, a spider and its web. But Mother said, "No."

Then one day Kotuka ran all the way home. "Mother, I do like school. Today the teacher put a microscope on the table." Kotuka described all the wonders he saw under the small, round glass. His mother said, "Wonders are all around you. You have only to use your bright eyes to discover them." Kotuka began that very day to find that what Mother said was true.

Judy told the children, "My father has a microscope. At his school his pupils look through it and see the wonders. He will bring it here, and we can see them too."

A page in the class book describes the visit.

Judy's father brought his microscope today. Everybody had a turn to look through the round glass. Richard looked first. He saw a hair that Betty had pulled out of her own head. "It looks like a big walking stick."

Larry looked first at the grain of salt. "Those little white blocks look like stacks of ice cubes."

Other things we looked at were a kernel of corn, a pink shell, a sliver of peanut, a piece of cotton cloth, dirt from one of our flower pots, and water.

Things in that water had all kinds of shapes. They were red and yellow and gray color. Ben, who looked first, said, "All those colors swimming around so fast look like strange zoo animals." Elsie thought they looked like fish darting around.

That microscope made us ask questions.

How can a brain know to make it?

How can its glass let us see what our eyes can't see?

Why don't we use our eyes more? Like every day and maybe find the answers for ourselves?

Did people, before there was a microscope, wonder what was inside a drop of water?

135

Or if a stone could grow?

Or how a seed grows and gets to be an apple good to eat?

We think they had to figure out a lot of things by themselves.

Kirk's mother and father also were willing helpers.

The calendar indicated the end of April. The class was talking about the May Day custom in many countries when children gather flowers, put them in bright baskets, hang them on the doors of friends' houses, then run away without being seen.

Beth remembered, "Leaving a secret May basket is like sending a secret message on Valentine Day. If I had a yard and flowers I'd make a May basket for you, Miss Ghetia, and for everybody in this class."

Kirk said, "You haven't got flowers. But I have. In Long Island where I live we're already getting dogwood blossoms on trees and flowers in our yard. My father and mother and my brothers and I can bring whole bunches."

When the teacher asked Kirk's parents if Kirk had let his interest in making baskets run away with him, they said, "Oh, no! Bringing flowers Sunday for May baskets is the nicest way of all to be needed." The next Sunday when two of Kirk's friends saw the family get out of the car with all the bunches of blossoms they asked Kirk, "Where did all the people sit?"

That day, when the "in order" teaching was completed, the contraband of imagination and fancy went into action. Flower stems were wrapped in wet paper, then in foil, and arranged in the colored paper cornucopia baskets with bright yarn handles. The bouquets, each different from all the others, were hurried to places like:

The door of the elevator, for their friend, the operator.

The top of the piano for the music teacher.

The lap of Miss Vernon, that day's visitor.

The door of the minister's study.

The room of Miss Henry, who one day had shared her autoharp music with them.

There were baskets, also, for taking home as surprises and for delivering to absent members.

Grandparents, too, respond favorably when grandchildren promise their services without proper consultation. The question in Claudia's class was: "What refreshments shall we have when our friends from Broome Street come to visit?" Claudia thought she knew the answer, "My grandmother in Toledo, Ohio, makes the *best* fudge. She'll tell us how to make it."

Their mouths watering in anticipation, the class dictated a letter. The recipe came. A committee, using money brought for sharing, bought the needed ingredients. Another committee worked in the kitchenette near the classroom and made the fudge. At home, Claudia wrote Grandmother and told her just how good it was and how much the visitors liked it.

Parents are people—professional people whose sharing sometimes extends beyond the immediate hour to be long remembered. Mr. Perry knew well the ways of children. He was the father of Daphne and Stephen. He also knew well the ways of the oboe. He played this instrument in a noted orchestra.

On the morning that he shared his music, he first took the instrument apart and held out the separate pieces for the children to see. He described the functions of each piece and talked about the wonder of its construction and of the tones the instrument could produce when its parts were put together again.

He talked about Beethoven, whose music he would play, the bright, happy days that should have been his because of his genius, and the dark, sad ones that came instead because of his deafness.

"In the *Pastoral* Symphony this great composer takes us on a visit to the country. To be out doors near birds, brooks, and growing things was his greatest happiness. Walking by himself in the woods, he would rest in the crotch of a favorite tree and sketch his musical ideas. This composition lets us feel as well as hear the wonder of the outdoors—light breezes stirring the leaves of trees, the ripples of gently flowing streams, tree branches bending and swaying rhythmically over the shining water.

"Then comes the call of the birds! When the whole orchestra plays this famous symphony, the flute brings the call of the nightingale. My little finger in this position on the oboe, repeats the note again and again, the piping of the quail. The clarinet plays the cuckoo's call.

"Listen now to these melodies with your heart as well as with your mind and ears. Someday, when you hear other instruments play them, you will remember them as friends.

"To create is a gift from the Creator. Both the creation of the music and of the instrument that brings it to us are marvels that make us all thankful."

Parents are people—people with many memories to share with children and who in sharing take the children with them into distant times and distant places.

Mr. and Mrs. Burke, teachers of a third grade, had a hunch about ways to use such a sharing before they met either the children or the parents. The class roll book started it.

"Here's a Dutch name."
"This one is Armenian, I'm almost sure."

"This one sounds Czech."

"This one sounds Polish."

"This one might be Scandinavian."

"Just think! Behind every name on this list there may be some happy childhood memory to share about Christmas in another land."

That very day one idea quickly followed another and a captivating plan began to take workable form. Subsequent home visits disclosed many of the suspected resources ready and waiting in the minds of particular parents, and plans for their use began to crystallize.

The parents, surprised and delighted with their part in these plans, began to anticipate the December sessions with as much eagerness as the children. And when the time came, they brought to those sessions a reality and uniqueness quite beyond the teachers' original hunch. They put into the minds and hearts of the children new and different Christmas scenes, new and different Christmas feelings.

On that first December day Peggy Ann's father led the way. The children, in imagination, walked with him and Peggy Ann along the quiet streets of Bethlehem. Past small, flat-roofed houses they went, and out to nearby hills. There they breathed the cool night air blowing across the olive trees. There they saw the shepherds tending their flocks, saw the star-filled sky, and talked of the baby born long ago in a shelter where the cattle rested because the inn in Bethlehem had no room for the family.

Then, with Martin's mother as storyteller and guide, they walked with her and Martin along the streets in the Czechoslovakian village where she had lived as a child. How pretty she looked today! How gay, wearing the bright-colored holiday blouse and skirt brought with other family treasures from that village. Holding imaginary lighted torches, the children joined other villagers in the climb to the small wooden church atop a high hill. There, in the midnight service they heard the Christmas story in words and music as Martin's mother remembered it. Then, with the other worshipers, they followed the winding path back to the village, calling out greetings of the glad New Day to neighbors and friends.

On another day, at the invitation of Joost's mother, the children went with her and Joost to their own home in Holland! With their own eyes they saw it in pictures Joost had made with his camera. What excitement in their city, for it was December 6, Saint Nicholas Day. And that good man himself would soon appear, coming by boat from Spain and riding a fine, white horse. Traveling with him would be his Moorish page boy, Black Piet, carrying a bag filled with gifts for the children.

"Will your Saint Nicholas wear a red suit and cap like our Santa Claus?" the children asked.

"Oh, no!" Joost's mother answered. "Our Dutch *Sinter Klaas* is a tall and stately figure. He wears a bishop's cloak and a tall miter-type hat, rising in a peak in front and back."

Then in more of Joost's pictures they saw Saint Nicholas and Black Piet, exactly as described. "And if you want to know what kind of gifts Black Piet brings in his bag, I'll tell you," said Joost. "Candy for good children and switches for bad ones."

"I'll bet I know what he left for you," teased Martin, but neither Joost nor his mother would tell.

Soon everyone learned the Saint Nickolas song and sang it merrily, not once but several times:

There comes in the distance a steamboat from Spain.
It brings us Saint Nick'las. We greet him again.
His horse is tripping all over the deck,
The pennants are blowing as bright as the flags.

Black Pietre is laughing. He warns us ahead,
Good children get candies, and bad ones a gad [switch].
Have mercy, Saint Nick'las, once more forgive.
We'll never be naughty as long as we live.

With Arthur's mother, joyful and Christmasy in her red full-skirted Armenian dress, the children in holiday mood also eagerly began their visit to her childhood home in Turkey. There with Arthur they helped prepare for the happy festival. In imagination they swept floors, then scrubbed them clean and shining. They washed curtains and spreads, making their colors bright again. They put every cupboard in order. They rolled out the dough and cut cookies into many shapes and sizes. Then—surprise! surprise!—they ate the real cookies that Arthur and his mother had baked and brought to them in holiday wrappings.

On another day Frederick's father taught the children to sing "Silent Night" in German. And David's father, from memories of his childhood in Norway, took them there to a small yellow house, like a spot of sun tucked among the trees high above the fjord. There, wearing heavy coats, mittens, caps, and boots, they went into the yard and helped David's grandfather tie a sheaf of grain to a stout pole kept year after year for that purpose. They slipped the pole deep into a hole that Grandfather had prepared and made it secure against heavy winds. The grain was the birds' feast for Christmas and for the many wintry days yet to come.

In a story the teacher told, the children were in India for Great Day. They helped sweep the courtyard clean, paint scenes from the Christmas story on the freshly whitewashed outer walls of the house, light the wicks in small clay lamps placed along walls of the courtyard and edges of the roof. The whole village aglow, travelers along the narrow country roads could find their way. Though the night might be dark, the lights of Christmas would guide them!

They were in Sweden, too, and heard the town band blow the Christmas in with lively music. They placed the friendly *Tomtar* (fairy elves), in red suits and caps, in the cave beneath the family's Christmas tree and awaited the coming of the good *Jula Gubben*.

On the globe map, brought by Laura's father, the travelers traced their many Christmas journeys, marking each country with a dot of colored paper. And the globe remained in the classroom for many weeks.

Yes, parents are people with more valuable and more varied contributions to offer than they themselves usually believe. The wise teacher, coveting the wealth of their talents, skills, and memories for his pupils, puts down his nets wherever he is, gently snares the riches, and pulls them in.

Sharing

"It's my heart and my love that makes me want to . . ."

Jerry, age 7

For one group of teachers, the results of their first staff meeting prior to the opening of church school were quite unexpected. One young, new teacher lost no time in speaking about the discussion topic, "Children's Growth."

Face aglow, she spoke out with conviction: "Frankly, I'm weary of the old refrain, 'Children's growth is the concern of every teacher.' What growth are we talking about? To me these words imply growth that is measured with a yardstick and scale, with answers that children correctly memorize and give back parrot-like to the teacher. Such growth holds no challenge for me. The growth I envision has quite different dimensions:

"*Hearts,* stretching east, west, north, south, encompassing other children with appreciative and loving concern.

"*Minds* eagerly seeking and finding new knowledge about these contemporaries so like yet unlike themselves.

"*Lives* putting something of themselves into other lives.

"*Hands* reaching, serving, sharing with them.

"Unless all of our teaching provides this kind of growing, tomorrow's world becomes the poorer because of our neglect."

When she finished, no one spoke. Yet in the silence minds were not stilled. Some turned back into memories. Others soared forward into new imaginings. In the resulting give-and-take of ideas and plans, belief in this urgent and important kind of growing took hold of each teacher and held fast. What matter earlier misgivings about how, when, where to start this new growing. Confidence, interest, commitment now gave assurance that ways would be found.

"After tonight," exclaimed one, "neither I nor my teaching will ever be the same!"

"And to think," marveled another, "it all started with ordinary words that we use every day. It's the way those words were arranged and spoken that makes the difference. They've inspired us, given us a blueprint."

"The mass media certainly confirm the need for this kind of growing," said another. "With the push of a button, children, parents, teachers, everybody sees the world scene. You name it—life, death, heartache, joy, poverty, riches . . . Asia, South America, the United States . . . any time of day or night. The point is, how do children *feel* about what they see? What do they *do* about it?"

144

"Or about what they read or hear," called out another, waving a paper taken from her handbag. "This, for instance: 'More than 3.3 billion fellow humans share this earth. One-sixteenth of this world family, blessed with luxury in the midst of world misery, are Americans.'"

Hastily making notes, another said, "Figures like these could start some growing. Put into a poster, children would quickly get the message. Some of these fellow humans are boys and girls on the mend in hospitals, children wanting books to read and games to play, items that hospitals seldom supply. Some are Navaho, Papago, and other Indian children attending schools on the reservations. Stored inside each pupil are countless pictures waiting to be expressed. But where are the paints, paper, brushes, the enthusiasm of teachers?"

Another said, "Church World Service must have charts and photographs showing areas in the world where our help is needed. I'll ask about them tomorrow."

"Plain lazy, that's me—in the past," confessed another. "Never a thought beyond what the lesson material suggested. Never a vote of confidence in the children to make their own plans about where and how to help. But watch it in the future! I'm changing all that."

"Remember," reminded the young teacher who had started it all. "Clues for encouraging this kind of growing are in every classroom. Put your antennae up. Tune in to what children say. Recognize the clues they give. But never predict the outcome."

For one class, the sharing of hearts and love began with Scott's announcement as he settled down to hear a Thanksgiving story. "What I'm thankfulest the most for is legs. Legs let me get where I want to go. They let me climb trees and run races and skate and ride my bike. Without legs I'd mostly just sit by the window and lie in bed."

Classmates probably began to think of similar deprivations and silently enumerated the pleasures their own legs provided, for all voiced agreement. Life without legs would indeed be tough.

Marian, ever the thoughtful one, observed, "You'd feel better about your tough deal if you knew you had friends who would figure out how to help you, like taking you for a ride or something."

Leonard, suddenly with an idea of his own, proposed, "Lets *us* find somebody that's crippled—I mean really crippled—and make him glad he's got us. Maybe the crippled hospital could tell us about a person like that."

Arthur's tug of interest sent him to consult the class money chart. A printed rhyme above the chart told about this fund.

> From the money given to us
> To save or spend or share,
> We bring gifts to send our friends
> And show them that we care.

"Ten dollars and eighty-two cents is OK for now," he reported. "It's really ten dollars and ninety-seven cents. I've just put in another dime and nickel. Everybody can bring more next week."

The *how* of getting the proposed gift being settled, the questions of *what* to get and *who* to receive it now claimed attention. Interest in the story of a past Thanksgiving was forgotten in their involvement with the present one.

In helping the group find answers to the two questions, the teacher introduced the words "orthopedic," "orthopedic hospital," and "children's social worker," explained the procedure for securing the desired information from the hospital, and offered to go for the interview before the next session. At that session everyone in the class was present and on time. They heard the following report:

"Eight-year-old Renee, born with two club feet, has been a longtime patient at the hospital. She first came there to receive a series of operations on the deformed feet and continues now as an outpatient, receiving periodic examinations and treatments.

"Renee lives in a housing project in Long Island, several miles from the hospital. Making the trip there is not easy for her. She has never been able to attend school, so a visiting teacher comes to her home each week.

"What Renee needs most is an afghan to spread over her lap when she sits by the window and to cover her at nap time. The social worker wonders if you could make this useful and needed gift. If so, she will share the plans with Renee's mother, but they will be kept secret from Renee. Well?"

"An afghan? Sure!"

"All we need are some weave-it frames."

"And some nice yarn, green."

The *what* and *who* now being settled, a committee, with the teacher, went shopping. Soon all kinds of fingers —stubby, awkward, quick, accurate—were working both in the classroom and at home. True, no completed square measured the exact size of another, but each represented its maker's best work. Interest seldom waned.

Scott's mother, caught up in the excitement of the finished squares (and possessing skill with a needle plus several hours of free time), offered assistance in completing Renee's gift. With Scott, Bill, and a steam iron as helpers, she coaxed the many woven squares into almost identical size, joined them with a pretty crochet stitch, then sewed the lining and border into place.

The following Sunday, children's eyes and hands approvingly examined the green coverlet displayed for a while on a classroom table before being wrapped for mailing.

"Just touching, you know it's pretty."

"Like from a real store."

Bill announced, "This afternoon, my family's going for a ride, and I think my father will ride me to Renee's house if I ask him. Then I could give her the box. Teddy can come with us if his mother lets him." Bill's extra interest in the afghan was understandable. Home from school for four days with a cold, he had worked overtime at weaving, thus topping the output of any classmate.

Other classes and teachers, having seen and admired the unusual gift and wanting to know its final chapter, were invited to hear the boys' report of their visit.

> Bill: My father had a hard time finding the right place. Out there the streets curve around, and we couldn't find any name.
>
> Teddy: Finally a man gave us directions. But when we found the street we couldn't find the house.
>
> Bill: We looked on a lot of buildings, but all the numbers were wrong. My father was wondering what to do. Then a lady came by and we told her the number we wanted. She said, "I'll show you."
>
> Teddy: It was right, too. I rang the bell.
>
> Bill: Renee's mother came, and when she saw us and the box she knew we had brought the surprise.
>
> Teddy: We went in, and Renee was at the table. She didn't know *anything*. I said, "I'm Teddy and he's

Bill and our class at church made you what's in the box."

Bill: She said, "Hello." And all of her began to smile. She held on to the box while her mother got the scissors.

Teddy: Renee wanted to do everything herself, and all of us got excited.

Bill: When she got the box open and saw what was inside, she took it out and just looked and looked.

Teddy: Then her mother held it up so she could see all of it good.

Bill: She kept on looking like she wouldn't ever stop. Then she said, "For me! I didn't know so many people loved me." She was about to cry. My father told us not to stay long because he was waiting. So we told her good-bye. She liked it. And us.

Another group's growing in the new way began the morning they found a strange box in their room. Alice read the printed enclosure: "A traveling exhibit of their paintings sent in friendship from children in Japan to children in the United States."

Quickly the bright paintings were providing a new look to the classroom that welcomed them.

Quickly excited children were telling each other, "These paintings are *good*."

Quickly a jubilant teacher was assuring himself, "A made-to-order way to meet face to face persons different from ourselves. To discover that we like them. To see some of the many things we have in common—eating, sleeping, playing, working, learning, growing, enjoying holidays. Why, out of that box has jumped the world's biggest concept—*brotherhood!*"

That very day paintings led to questions, questions led to books. In another week books began to lead to an assortment of activities and to growing in ways the teacher had anticipated.

Singing a song in Japanese words.

Playing a Japanese game.

Listening to "One-Inch Fellow," a favorite Japanese story.

Learning to count to ten and to say "Good morning" and "Thank you" in Japanese.

Imagining attending Girls' Day Festival and Boys' Day Festival.

What else they would lead to no one could have guessed.

Meanwhile, sad but true, the exhibit must keep its schedule.

"Unpacking was fun. Packing isn't. I'm used to the pictures. I wish we could keep one."

"Me too. Who wants empty walls?"

Kingsley said, "We could make them some pictures telling about us. We wouldn't be copycats if we wrote stories about the pictures and put everything in a book instead of an exhibit."

A wail sounded: "But I can't paint *that* good, like theirs."

"So take pictures with your camera," Kingsley said.

A second wail: "What about me? I can't paint, and I haven't got a camera."

"Then use your allowance and buy postcard pictures," said Kingsley.

Kingsley's proposals began to catch on, to seem workable, and to be good ideas. Once again pictures began to cover classroom walls. *Photographs* showing children and teacher in many places—in the classroom, beside the church door, in the playground.

Postcard pictures showing favorite places the children knew in the city—Statue of Liberty, United Nations, Empire State Building, Natural History Museum.

Their *own paintings* and drawings showing themselves

inside and outside their apartment homes, at the zoo, going to school, skating on the sidewalks, riding on the subway.

Each child wrote a story to match each of his pictures. The teacher typed them. Mounted on uniform-size pages and arranged in sequence, the picture storybook pleased everyone.

Several months after the book had been mailed to the children in Japan, the long-awaited letter of acknowledgment was received. But it was not from the children. It bore the signature of a teacher in the high school.

> . . . So your book to the children is now my book. It is my best textbook. With it I teach your English language to Japanese pupils. With it, I also teach about your city.

> Pupils read the stories many times and are understanding. Pupils also look many looks at the pictures and learn everyday something new.

> Pupils and teachers like your book. It is fine textbook. It tells and shows what other books not tell and show.

> *Arigato!* I thank you.

The children—textbook writers! They could hardly believe it.

Mrs. Mueller was the children's friend. Wearing a fresh white apron, she left on their table each week a tray holding a pitcher of milk, cups, graham crackers, and paper napkins. One day she told Manya and Ruth, "I like coming to your room. In here I think of Elsa. She's just your age, just your size."

The teacher, hearing, invited, "Please stay some morning and tell us about Elsa. Could she come and visit us?"

The next week Mrs. Mueller stayed for a while. "This is Elsa," she said, handing some pictures in turn to the children gathered around her. "My sister in Germany adopted her. Now my sister has a little daughter, and I am an auntie. Germany is too far to travel, so I have never seen Elsa. I know her only through pictures and the letters my sister writes.

"Here Elsa is playing with her kitten. Here she and her mother are in the park. Here she is wearing the dress and ribbons I sent for Christmas. My sister's husband has been sick for a long time, and I help in this way whenever I can. Elsa makes all of us happy. Children around the world do that for mothers and fathers and aunties."

There were questions about Elsa's house, her school, games she played, if she had brothers and sisters. That Elsa spoke a language different from their own was a surprise.

"Could one of Elsa's pictures stay here?" asked Ruth. "Then she would belong to our class."

The teacher added, "We would put the picture here on the board. Then she will always be waiting for us and welcome us when we come." Mrs. Mueller liked this plan, so pictured Elsa became friend Elsa.

In time, the children turned some of their offering money into a dress for Elsa. Mothers, knowing about Elsa, discovered at home dresses, ribbons, woolen stockings, and mittens the right size for her and put them in boxes with her name. Two fathers, seeing the boxes in the classroom, found Mrs. Mueller and told her, "Elsa's boxes are much too heavy for you to carry. We will take them to the post office for you."

Mrs. Mueller nodded. "I know. So many good wishes are packed inside. So many kindnesses. Elsa and I never could count all of them."

In another class first one child and then another exclaimed, "Our play's good!" Of course it was good. Hadn't they created it from a favorite story "The Three Camels"? Hadn't Miss Elsie Spriggs written it? Weren't all of her stories good?

Neither children nor teacher had met Miss Spriggs. But knowing her stories they knew her, also. They especially liked "The Three Camels." It took them across the world to a toy shop in India. It provided a story person for every child to become.

"Danny can be the shopkeeper and take the money."

"Doug's OK to be Tom."

"George's father's a doctor. Let George be Tom's father. *He's* a doctor."

"All the people who buy toys have to look interested and have their money ready."

Many of the toys needed for the shop the children brought on loan from home—a jump rope, drum, horns, blocks, dolls, balls, balloons, a little wagon. These and the several that they made were arranged on the various shelves of the shop. For everybody, the favorites of all the toys were the three camels made by the children. These—the large one, the middle-sized one, the small one—they placed to stand together on the lowest shelf. Here the village children who came to buy could easily see them—could easily reach out and touch them. Here at play-practice time the class could look and admire.

"They're cute."

" 'Specially the littlest. I wish I could take it home."

"We shoulda made more camels."

"Stupid. The play's only got *three* camels."

The play's audience watched with interest as the story unfolded before them. Scene I showed the toy shop. Villagers, old and young, choosing and buying the toys.

The patient shopkeeper, answering the many questions. Selling the large camel. Selling the middle-sized camel. What? Shop-closing time and the littlest camel left alone on the shelf?

Scene II, the following afternoon, brought the living room of Tom's home into view, with a Christmas tree, Tom, and his friend Sita. Then, how fast the play's action. A sudden turn of events, and the play was over. Contented sighs from the audience signaled their delight that, at last, everything was as it should be.

There, before them on the living room wall, they saw a picture of three camels being guided by three kings following a bright star in the night sky. On a bench beneath the picture, the three toy-shop camels stood side by side—large, middle-sized, small. Dancing around the tree were Tom, Sita, and their new friend they met for the first time just minutes ago. Tom's father had brought her from the hospital to share Tom's Christmas. Once very ill, the little girl now was much better. In her arms when she came was the small camel—bought and given to her that day by the hospital nurses.

The play over, members of the audience approached the low stage and greeted the children. One visitor patiently awaited her turn. "You do not know me," she said. "But I know your story very well. So I say one thank-you for myself and one for my good friend Elsie Spriggs, for you have made her story people seem very real. Last month I was in England and saw my friend in her home. She is ill. In the letter I am writing to her this afternoon I will describe your toy shop, the three camels, Tom's Christmas tree. She can see them, too. Good-bye, now. You must play her stories often."

Turning, the visitor walked toward the door. In the hall, Tom, Sita, and the thin little girl from the hospital suddenly were there beside her, each holding out a camel—the large one, the middle-sized one, the small one.

"They're for her."

"Send them, please, with your letter."

"On a shelf by her bed, they'll be her company."

They were, for the remaining weeks that she lived.

Shirley's enrollment in the class began a series of adventures in sharing that continued through the year and eventually touched every child in six classes.

Shirley could not see with her eyes. She went to a special day school. She used a pencil that was different. She played anagrams with letters marked in a special way. Shirley was special.

In time the inevitable questions came.

"Why can't we visit Shirley's school?" "And meet the friends in her school class?" "And make her class a present?"

In time a conference brought answers to the questions. "Yes, please come visit Shirley's class and play games with them. They especially like puzzle toys."

Jigsaws began to cut the puzzles. To cut a wooden circle into five pie-shaped wedges. To cut a rectangle into six straight-edged pieces of different sizes. To cut a square into four triangular-shaped pieces. To cut a triangle into four straight-edged pieces of different sizes.

Sandpaper began to make the many wooden pieces smooth.

Children, blindfolded, began to discover whether or not their work was well done. Were edges smooth? Had even one rough place gone unnoticed? Did all puzzle pieces fit together easily?

Meanwhile, two members of the class reported seeing

and following a seeing-eye dog as he guided his master in the neighborhood.

"How does a dog learn to guide?"

"Is the master ever scared the dog might make a mistake? Might forget?"

"Why can't we invite a dog to visit us and bring his master? Then we could find out about everything."

In time such a visit was arranged. Other classes, now also interested in the occasion, helped prepare questions for the dog's master to answer and helped extend a welcome to the two guests. There were many questions.

"Mister Frank, how did you know to take only two steps to get on the platform?"

"What kind of dog is Buddy?"

"Who told you how to take care of him, like giving him a bath?"

"Why doesn't Buddy bark with so many people getting so close to him?"

"I think Buddy's sense is better than people's sense."

"Could we come to the seeing-eye place and see where you got Buddy?"

In time the results of another conference were known. "Yes, please come to Seeing Eye and see for yourselves the new owners getting acquainted with their guide dogs and getting accustomed to handling them. See also the trainers training the dogs to be the guides."

Teachers, children, parent-drivers—eight cars full—made the trip to Morristown, New Jersey, watched the activities taking place in the yards and along the pathways. The children's report to those unable to go was interesting and complete. Then another inevitable question, coming this time not from one class but from six. "Why can't we buy a dog for somebody who needs one?"

No project, once conceived, seems impossible to children, not even after they discover the cost. And this group of children discovered that guide dogs are *very* expensive. Each class counted its own accumulated offering money. It was not enough. More was needed. Each child brought more and more.

In another five weeks, at year's end, dollars, half-dollars, quarters, dimes, nickels, pennies were counted again. A jubilant committee reported the sum. "Enough for half a dog!"

So it was. The following day a check was on its way to the Seeing Eye. For years the children wondered and asked, "Which half of the dog did we buy?" No one ever knew.

There is no one way to promote world understanding, world friendliness. The ways and range are as diverse as the imaginations of the children and teachers can devise.

In a city that includes people of many cultures, races, and religions, exchange visits between groups of children not only become the basis for understanding, appreciation, and friendliness today, but also prepare the participants for living happily together as responsible adults tomorrow.

An exchange of letters and pictures between groups within one country or several brings unexpected and lasting rewards, for children are world-minded in their thinking and outreach and have much to share with each other.

Books that present stories and illustrations of persons living in unfamiliar parts of one's own country and in countries far distant from it, plus conversations with friendly travelers knowledgeable about those persons and places, can also contribute to children's growth.

Both in living rooms and classrooms such books and conversations are able to correct distorted ideas, minimize differences, emphasize similarities, and give a one-world feeling. When this happens the growing children are on their way to becoming adults who will live in harmony and contentment with neighbors near and far.

Children who begin early to feel and to understand the humanness and worth of all peoples and who learn to add something of themselves to every relationship with others are making a start toward becoming flexible adults who will accept changing times and ways, gracefully adjust to them, and create useful lives of fulfillment for themselves and their families in whatever homeland they happen to be.

The result of today's growth in children is not to be calculated today. Nor can it be measured next week or next year. Perhaps by the year 2000 it can be reckoned, for by then the children of today's world will have become the parents, neighbors, friends, teachers, planners, leaders of tomorrow's world. And the kind of world they bring into existence then will depend largely on the kind that, as children, they are encouraged and permitted to make today.

When "my heart and my love" are generously shared today no one can say how far into the twenty-first century their influence will be seen and felt.

Bibliography

Allstrom, Elizabeth. *Let's Play a Story.* New York: Friendship Press, 1957.

Barkan, Manuel. *Through Art to Creativity.* Boston: Allyn & Bacon, 1960.

Behn, Harry. *Chrysalis: Concerning Children and Poetry.* New York: Harcourt, Brace & World, 1968.

Colum, Padraic. *Story Telling New and Old.* New York: Macmillan, 1968.

D'Amico, Victor. *Creative Teaching in Art.* Scranton, Pa.: International Textbook, 1942.

Fryatt, Norma R., ed. *A Horn Book Sampler: On Children's Books and Reading.* Boston: Horn Book, 1959.

Gaitskell, Charles D. *Children and Their Art.* New York: Harcourt, Brace & World, 1958.

Gezari, Temima. *Footprints and New Worlds.* New York: Jewish Education Press, 1964.

Jacobs, Leland B., ed. *Using Literature with Young Children.* New York: Teachers College Press, 1965.

Lewis, Richard, ed. *Miracles: Poems by Children of the English-speaking World.* New York: Simon and Schuster, 1966.

Lowenfeld, Viktor, and Brittain, W. Lambert. *Creative and Mental Growth*. New York: Macmillan, 1964.

Petty, Walter, and Bowen, Mary. *Slithery Snakes and Other Aids to Children's Writing*. New York: Appleton-Century-Crofts, 1967.

Richardson, Elwyn S. *In the Early World*. San Francisco: Tri-Ocean Books, 1964.

Sawyer, Ruth. *The Way of the Storyteller*. New York: Viking Press, 1962.

Shedlock, Marie. *The Art of the Story-Teller*. New York: Appleton-Century-Crofts, 1956.

Siks, Geraldine Brain. *Creative Dramatics: An Art for Children*. New York: Harper & Row, 1958.

Slade, Peter. *Child Drama*. London: University of London Press, 1954.

Swenson, May. *Poems to Solve*. New York: Charles Scribner's Sons, 1966.